Adventures in the High Wind
Poetic Observations and Other Lore

Robert Nichols

Mountain Muse Publishing
Lincoln City, Oregon

Adventures in the High Wind (E-edition 2013)
by Robert Nichols

Cover design and art: Robert Nichols

First Printing 1990
Second Printing (e-publishing) 2013
Third Printing (BOD) 2917
Illustrated by: Albert Dreher, Robert Nichols

Mountain Muse Publishing
P.O. Box 406
Lincoln City, OR 97367
MtMusePublishing.com

ISBN Number: 0-9627615-0-8
E-book ISBN Number 0-978-0-9627615-6-0

Dedicated to:

Robert Lee Nichols (1914 – 2011)
my father, my friend

Table of Contents

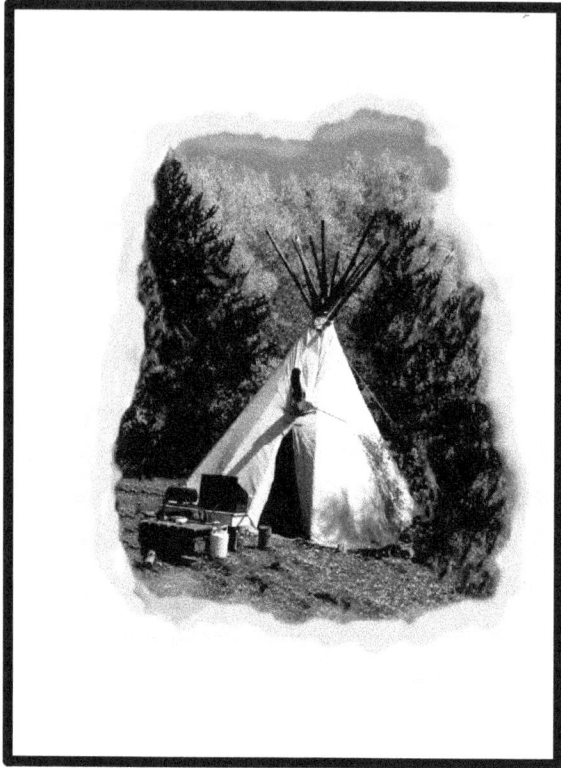

Summer 1990
Park County, Colorado

Words, the Wind... the Adventure Continues

May 31, 2013

I worked on this book most of the summer of 1990. It was up in Park County, Colorado, during a five-year period when I had my tipi camp on the edge an aspen grove overlooking Cowboy Flats. Actually, I started gathering my poems and 'lore' from new and old notebooks and footlockers and coat pockets throughout the good long winter before.

At a Rocky Mountain elevation of nearly ten thousand feet, powerful storms would settle in on me for raging days and blizzard-shrouded nights. And, when it would clear off to sub-zero clarity, myriad stars would spin the night in galactic wonder all about me. I loved those seasons, those years in mountain's embrace. I wrote a poem about it.

Tipi Nights: Winter

Deep winter night.
An enticing shimmer of fear and cold
enveloped me as,
crouching through the low doorway,
I departed the warm-lit wrap of the Tipi.

Hermit times they were,
 dwelling far up the side
of a distant mountain,
alone
but for the invisible warriors
whose wind-whispered
taunts and urgings
called me to check the night
before sleep.

With these ghosts of the wilds

as my spirit companions,
in a ritual
that spun centuries
down to the essence
of a single night,
and spun
a single night
back out
to all the scatter of centuries,
I circled my camp
in final communion
with moon
and stars
and clouds of coming weather.

We paused
in the snowfield spill of the moon—
my spirit friends, myself,
and all the motions of time and
distance—
thrilling to the chill
of pure winter night,
(how the fabric glowed white
against the lightless curtain of the forest—
this cone of stick and canvas
I called my home)
and in stillness we listened for danger.

The flap secured,
the fire set back to a good long glow,
the hissing lantern silenced—
in darkness, beneath wool blankets,
as the cold worked
against the dampened woodstove,
I touched the stock of my shotgun,
pulled my knit cap tightly upon my head,
settled in,
and, suspended there,
raptly absorbed by the absolute stillness,
glad in the closeness of mortal truth...

I deeply breathed a fresh good
breath of God's Universe
and shattered the immense quiet
with laughter!

Yes, I relished the grit and challenge, the ridiculous liberation of those reckless times in the realm of raw blessing and mortal risk. There are Gods who live where only holy hermits and madmen would dare to dwell. You know, damn-fool poets and the like. And don't ever confuse the Gods of the natural world with your Fairy Godmother. The undiluted spiritual essence of a winter's night miles from the nearest human is a wonder to know but never to trifle with. God's love is an opportunity, not a promise. Sometimes it would get so dark up there—and I'm not talking about long nights of the cold solstice or unrelenting lightless cloaks of cloud and swirling snow— sometimes just being a poet dwelling in the unguarded recesses of his own mind was so bereft of glimmers of safety that I would just give it up and make the sixty-mile run down the switchbacks and stream-course highways into town and camp out on the living room couch of my best friend and often wife Carol.

You see, this matter of living a life of art is dangerous.

Those times up on the mountain with my solar panel electric system, my little Toshiba laptop computer, a single 12V light bulb and all the expanse and explosion of Cosmic reality a-swirl about me, I was living the metaphor that is the title of this work. I was having an adventure in an actual high wind—that's for sure. But a poem's power is not in the accuracy of its depiction of reality. Power comes with leaps of poetic language arcing words into magical never-realms of mutual experience. I lived the metaphor of wind and danger, but my poetry is of an open encounter with the creative might of God-sized Art. It was physically harrowing to confront gale-rushing tempests and extremes of cold and isolation in the wilds, but these poems do not tell of wind and threat, they tell of the sense of peril that is universal to all who open minds and hearts to the fullness of life.

Which brings us up to this spring day in 2013. I live in a real house, have rejoined my wife Carol in our lifelong journey together, have the love and belief of our daughter Kristin to lift and encourage my days and, yet, knowing what I do of the nature of Art, I am as awash in the deadly splendor of this singing Universe as ever I was in rage and wonder of the high mountains.

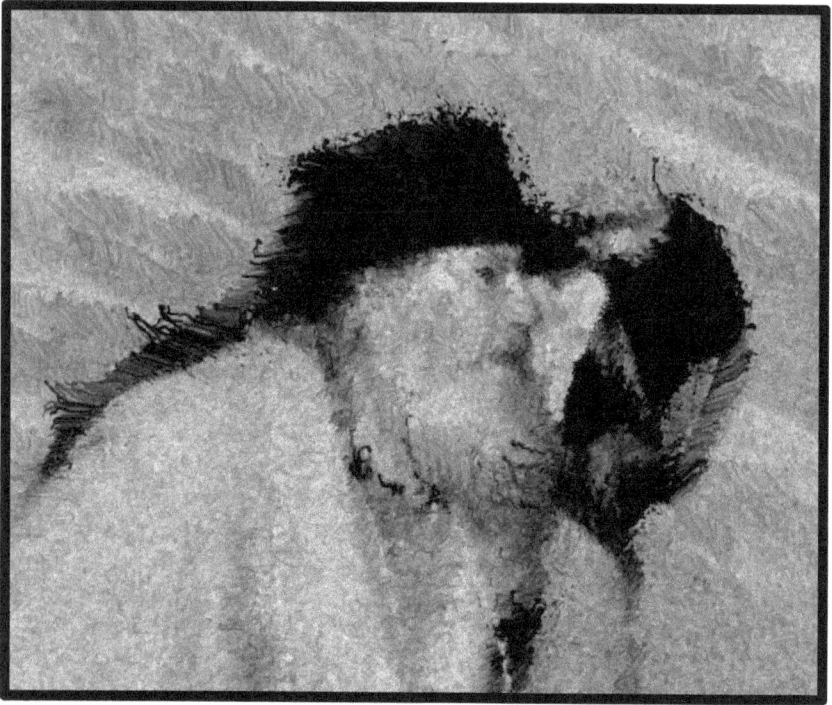

Robert, playing the fool out on the edge of Ever.
Hey, if we're not laughing
(with the Gods, or with ourselves)
then aren't we just wasting our time here?

A New Poem for an Old Book

I should begin this new edition of my book of "Poetic Observations and Other Lore" with a new poem, don't you think?

Poetry and a Good Song Sung

Song and metaphor drive this good day.
Nothing so real that can't be
better known, better expressed
(in-your-gut,
soul-spun
deeply, sweetly
heart-suffered)
by words poetic:
shouted,
sung,
laughed like an ocean,
wept like autumn drizzle,
whispered like promised love,
read like lines of a face
(raging or about to smile),
like lips wanting kiss,
rage vying revenge,
child giggles teasing tickle—
    lines of a soul-spoken moment,
    eternal and ever fleeting.

Leaps of imagination
and startling quirks of irony. Yes!
Cleanly choreographed
rhymes and meters. Yes!
Artful streams of consciousness—
like spilling rivers,
coursing mind journeys
to exotically mundane

ports of
home sweet love,
frightful honesty,
desperate joy.

Ever been there?

No place for the weak of heart, you know.
Flowers do not decorate,
they explode holy beauty.
And songs do not sedate,
they lightning-bolt, jig-dance
the wonder-stunned mind;
they sorrow-course the blood
with merciless swells of emotion.
And the heart is not flesh.
    The heart is the poetic core
    of human essence.

It is such a story,
this poem of life.
Recited in roared and whispered rush
of truth
known only by honest passion,
rapt attention,
and
(care-be-damned),
a risk-frenzied willingness
to feel full force
the hilarity, the curse of its blessings,
real and magical,
to the very bone of being.

It is a poem,
purely, simply
a poem we live, we sing,
we marvel to know.

Like "Little Bo Peep who lost her sheep,"
and love like "a summer's day"
and raging the "rage against the dying of the light"

and a Raven speaking doom.

And a grocery list where "deli meats"
rhymes with "sweet candy treats."
And the meter of raindrops
on roof tops
says it all,
every never word of it.

And the song:
just take the beat of your heart
and, for melody,
the secrets of a woodland path,
and all the metaphoric mystery
of the stretching Universe drawing
upon the notice of your
simple mortal wonder,
and sing this poem of life with me.
Oh, dear friend,
let us sing it together.

(Spring, 2013)

Albert Dreher / 1990

8

Introduction

Think of it as a High Wind.

A Force that blows across the Universe scattering the night-burning stars.

A Force of such beauty and power that no mortal being can possibly bear to stand fully before it without being torn forever from this Earth.

Think of this High Wind as being the creative energy of the Cosmos.

It is the omnipotent Source of all the enlightenment of the human spirit and, just as it has scattered the stars, it, too, has scattered the souls of a million poets into the infinite chill of the Void—a million poets and artists and musicians and all manner of others who have attempted to know its Power, its Beauty, and have recklessly dared to brave too much of its might.

(And you thought Dylan Thomas drank himself to death.)

The High Wind is the raw energy of a reality far more vast than our frail flesh can fully experience.

It is the breath of a Truth that dwarfs the petty, man-gods to whom we cast our crude and desperate prayers.

It is the deadly allure of Art.

Hunker down in the leeward calm of comfort's shelter and you will only faintly hear its howling call.

Stand slightly aloft of such complacent safety and, for a while, know with me the precarious world of the poet's earthly grasp and celestial dare.

Join me in these Adventures in the High Wind.

Here's to You

I am a poet—an honest speaker of a human vision.

I am not a romance-book man. I have lived the trash and turmoil of soap operas—we all have. I will not be a teller of such shallow-hearted foolishness and superficial eroticism.

I am not a humor-book man. In New York, where accountants and lawyers and other merchants determine what is the literary culture of an entire nation of readers, there are only inside jokes, and I shall always be an outside person.

I am not a holy-book man. My God is the wonder-vicious Creative Wind that would blow me from the face of existence were it not for careful anchoring upon the earth by the desperate embrace of love. My God is hardly the stuff of moral dilemma and personal damnation.

I am not a pornographer-man for I have loved women, and I yet love women.

I am no fact-man. For me there is little fascination to the grounding distraction of certainty.

By the commercial and material measure of the practical world in which I live, I am not a successful writer.

Rather, I am a poet who will tell his stories and times to any who will listen.

Through these poems, written sketches, and stories—real and imagined, I have written of places I have traveled, people I have encountered, and energies I have sensed emanating from the spirit of existence. They are not ramblings of fondled fantasies selfishly reconstructed from the complexity and ruin of my days, nor are they furtive expressions of my singular gleaning of bitterness. These words were not written for myself.

I once wrote: Artists do not keep secrets; artist tell them.

Poets do not create poetry when they write only for themselves.

I have written these words for you, World.

You, people,

You, Person.

And for $10.00 and whatever time you can spare them, they are yours.

Patience

He waits with his senses wide open—
soul spread to the fickle, chilled day.
(Snow flurries pass the window
drifting down from the sky, white-gray.)

And he knows no certain coming
of the warmth and life it should bring,
yet he waits with his fortieth March
for the birth of his fortieth spring.

(1984)

Words from the Last Condominium

I had such a beautiful poem to write—
one full of rich vibration and flowing truth,
a touch of dread,
a subtle lift of hope.
But I made the mistake of opening
the drapes and looking out beyond
the railing of my third-story balcony
at the ruined world spread before me—
a smoldering, tangled horror
engulfed by a pall of black smoke,
and the poem,
in embarrassment,
slipped away to silence.

Writing poems was like waiting
for the phone to ring,
so, I closed the drapes
and, curling up beneath a tattered quilt
upon the last couch,
I shut my burning eyes
and laughed the muttered laugh of a madman
until I slept;

And then the phone rang.

I answered it.
"I thought everyone was dead," I said.
"Not quite," came the answer.
"Would you like to hear a poem?" I asked.

The Gathering

I have known a flat and empty time
when seldom were there wind-songs or rain-rhythms,
a time of chill without the lucid touch of winter's cold,
a time of sex without the giddy shiver of love,
a place of shelter without the ember-glowing heat
of my own soul:
A cold time
in which the passing of days
was only the passing of moments,
only the passing of life.

But, also,
I have known the memory-shuddered voice
of tree-gusted autumn,
the wet-tapped telling of spring storms
playing musically upon the pale green infancy of
April leaves,
I have known the sound and sensation of morning—
laughing with sunrise-glow upon sweat-creased sheets
and singing naked secrets blessed by the caress
of love's hazy dawning eyes.
I have known the sanctuary of belief
against the inquisition of self-doubt:
I have known the beating of a heart
filled with the joyous, soul-deep breath
of my own life.

So now,
as the dance and doldrums of my times
envelop successive days with their separate
and sometime gentle, stifling, scintillating array
(knowing only what the raging storms know
of the winds that glide them wildly across
the reach of the sky),
I live the cycles of my times

with patience born of perception
of the spring-breath warmth
of mountain-drafted winter winds melting
the stolid face of January
with hints of May;
born of recollection of nights of slashing,
fervent-oathed fury
relenting to the tear-cleared eyes
of a new day's forgiveness;
born with the truth of the ever-mysterious wonder
of each fulfillment of today
despoiling the doom of yesterday's prophets.
A patience
heeding the respiratory pace
of seasons breathing upon sacred seasons,
paced by the drum of the human heart predominant
in the symphony of existence,
of patience measuring the steady might
of the rhythms of years
over the frenzied arrhythmia
of the gifts and the terrors of moments.

And the empty time,
flat and chilled,
will haunt again, in seeping persistence,
the soul-scattered, desperate abandonment
of bleak and artless days;
but, also again—
with song of cloud-drawn season sung resonantly
through the once muted fibers of my being—
will the full-felt times of
variegated fascination make rich
the epoch of my passage.

Each life in spiraling cycles
collects
all the moods and passions,
all the beauty and boredom,
love and vacancy;
all matters caressed and brutally collided—
all the dust-settled, dreary days,

all the wild and child-free flying days,
all the subtle, silent days.
And each life, a mosaic of all moments,
each life is a gathering.

When Van Gogh Has Taught Me How to See

When Van Gogh has taught me how to see,
to speak the shades, shadows, textures,
and tints of flesh and far flung stars;

when Beethoven has taught me how to hear,
to chorus the vibrant airs of the human spirit,
the bombastic heights of human triumph
and fragile rage,
the melodious themes of the singing soul;

when life's pulsing blood-truth has taught me
its touching energies, its love-secret caresses,
its bludgeon-scarred survival,
its death and its birth…

then, perhaps, I will begin to know words
for the wonders of my times
and will write the colors of this autumn—
haunting with deepening memory
the aura of these chilling days:
these desperate, holy moments of my own heart.

Appalachian Symphony

May 5, 1989. Oak Hill, West Virginia,
(Aunt Margie's house) 7:15 a.m.

Spring has come late and fitfully
to the Appalachians this year,
settling with full flourish in deep valley pockets
where fresh-leaved oak trees commence
the processes of summer,
while ignoring chilled, steep slopes
and wind-raw ridges
where other oaks are only sparsely coloring
in the hint of life's emergence
from the stark strength of their dark limbs reaching.
And, regardless of spring's fickle caress,
throughout the random poetry of the wildlands
in metaphor with wintry wood
or lyric harmony with verdant glade
dogwoods are flowering white.

And, from the hillside vantage
of my Aunt Margie's front porch,
where grassy fields and careful lawns
and tall-treed thickets fall gently
toward the waking town,
and distant mountains are all but lost
to the mist and the steadily falling rain,
I watch and listen.

My coffee steams in the moist chill of the morning air.
A robin watches from the wet sidewalk.
In spraying sighs cars pass by upon the country road.

In this symphony of early morning,
the woodwind birds flute and piccolo
and distantly

a single solemn mourning dove oboes a haunting
counter to the chirping variations
upon a theme of nature's lusting appetites.
Far down the falling valley
freight trains rumble percussion.
And all about me, in ineffable sweep,
vibrato, straining strings
sing the virile energies of life.

As I sip my honey-sweetened coffee
and absorb the crescendo of this mellifluous moment
of birdsongs, rain patter,
and the beating of my own heart,
the ever-dissonant tones and distractions
of reality's wars and debts and impossibilities
are made mute by the might of the song.

Aunt Margie on her front porch, Spring, 2000

The Victory

I got home from high school and I was angry. I didn't really know why I was angry. The immediate cause meant little anyway. It was a quiet, persistent anger, and nobody other than myself knew of its existence. My brother-in-law, he's my ex-brother-in-law now, was sitting at the kitchen table and he looked smug as usual. I had never seen him when he wasn't smirking. He was just sitting there and my mom was nervous and my sister had tears in her eyes and the little kid, my nephew, was being quiet so I knew it had been a hell of a scene I had just missed.

And all my brother-in-law said was, "Want to arm wrestle?"

"Sure," I said.

He'd been in the army and had hustled pool and sold used cars and I was just a "C" student in my last year of high school but I told him "sure." Losing wasn't that big of a deal anyway, and, by damn, it sure would have felt good to have beaten that cocky bastard, if for no other reason, just for my sister and for my mom who looked so tense. I was glad Dad wasn't there yet. If he'd been there nothing would have happened out in the open—it would have all been kept secret like always: my sister hurting, my mom worrying, and my brother-in-law making everyone as miserable as he was.

Nobody tried to interfere either. My mom and my sister just sat back and looked at me and at him like maybe we would resolve something that all of them hadn't even begun to touch with their sporadic outbursts of pent-up pain and its confusing truth.

Things were really getting more important than they should have been. I just threw my coat on the sofa and sat down across one corner of the kitchen table from him. He never quit smirking but he wasn't a bad person—just young. Too damn young to be a father and a husband and a used car salesman all at the same time. Somewhere in the mix of the desires and the responsibilities and the dollars, he must have started feeling lost and that was probably why he was smirking all the time and being cruel to my sister and hiding his fear.

In arm wrestling, usually you either win or you lose. One wrist weakens and bends and then it's all over. Every now and then, though, it doesn't work that way. Once in a while nobody moves in either direction, no wrist starts to bend. Sometimes it's so even that there's a stalemate with both guys full out and nobody moving either way. Then you just have to wait for one person to start hurting too much to go on or just to give up.

That's the way it was with my brother-in-law and me. We gripped hands and stared across at each other. And then he said "Go!" and, to the surprise of both of us, nothing happened. Well, it's hard to say "nothing" when every muscle in your body is pulling in one direction. But, in terms of results, nothing was happening. As soon as I realized he wasn't going to smash me right away, I started thinking seriously about winning. Mom and my sister moved closer to us when nothing happened.

"Say, brother-in-law," he said to me. "This comes as a real shock. I didn't know you were this strong."

"That makes two of us who are surprised," I said with the least amount of gasping possible so as to seem calm and confident in the situation.

"What do you mean, 'two of us,' Brother?" he said with what sounded like equal strain to me.

"You're surprised I'm this strong," I said with a voice of squeezed wind, "and I'm surprised you're this weak."

Sometimes it takes a long time to realize the full impact of the viciousness of our own little jokes.

"We'll see about that," he said, and I felt the anger rising in his strength.

Then my sister spoke for the first time since I had gotten home. She didn't speak loudly, but what she said came from her heart. All she said, and it was a whisper spoken just to me, all she said was, "Don't let him beat you. Don't let him."

I heard what she said. I'm sure he did, too. I could feel it in his wrist.

It was really starting to hurt. I could feel the muscles of my right arm begin to cramp from the continued strain.

"Hey, Mom," he said to my mother, wasting more of his tight air. "I hear she's against me now; who are you rooting for?" And then he nearly choked on a dark chuckle.

"Take him, take him," my sister was telling me from the sorrow of the obvious mistake of her marriage.

My arm was really hurting by then.

21

"Come on, Mom," he said through forced air. "Join the crowd. Make it unanimous. Get me. Get me."

It was all so distorted. A simple contest of strength had taken on such exaggerated significance. But, by then, there was no getting out of it.

"You want to quit?" I said. "Call it even?"

Then he said what I knew he would say, "Never, Brother-in-law, never."

And he said more. "It'll never be even again."

My sister needed me to win.

My mother hated it all so much.

The kid played with his little toys in the center of the living room rug far, far away, and, yet, so close.

"You want to give up?" my brother-in-law asked.

"No," I said but, hell yes, I did. It hurt so bad in my arm—as though the stress was tearing away its insides. And it hurt so bad to see my sister there with her love turned to such hatred; it hurt so bad to see my mother and feel her helplessness; and it even hurt to see my brother-in-law so absolutely wrong and, at the same time, so absolutely alone.

No one said anything for a long time, or at least it seemed to be a long time to me. He would move an inch his way, and from somewhere I'd come up with enough energy to pull him back up and sometimes even a touch beyond straight up. But neither of us seemed to be close to summoning enough strength to bend the other's wrist and win. It was going to be even until an arm gave out, or until one of us gave in.

With an abrupt opening of the front door, my father walked into the bizarre scene. It must have been quite a sight for him. After twenty-five miles of fighting rush-hour traffic from the city to our comfortable suburb, he wandered into a battlefield in his own kitchen. There was my brother-in-law on one side of the table, flushed with strain, and me across from him just as bad off; and Mom and my sister hovering about the both of us with such anxiety and dark hopes.

"What's going on here?" demanded my father.

No one said a word. My sister just kept on with her, now silent, desperate encouragement for my victory. My mom didn't say anything, but it was clear how much she had been holding in for so long. And he and I were beyond talking or fighting or pulling—we were just hurting until one of us finally would hurt too much.

Dad walked over to the table and he knew what was going on but he said it again anyway, "What's going on here?"

And then my bother-in-law's smirk eased up for an instant, and he damn near grinned at me. Not like people grin when something is half way funny or you've heard a little joke—he grinned the heart-empty turning of a face lost from itself.

I think I did too.

It was an unspoken signal. We both carefully let up in equal amounts—God how it hurt—until our hands were free of each other's.

The women sighed. My mom went back to her cooking; my sister went into the living room and sat down on the floor next to the kid; my father went upstairs to change out of his business suit; and, within a couple of days, my brother-in-law had packed up and had left us all forever.

No wrist had bent, no arm had fallen, no apparent victor had emerged from the conflict. But now, so many years later, I know that I lost. It was a contest, not of strength or endurance (on those grounds we were equally weak), but rather of tolerance to pain and in our stalemate he had borne so much more than I. There was no way in the sheltered time of my seventeen-year-old eyes I could have begun to have shown the pain that emanated from my ex-brother-in-law's eyes as he listened to the words of my sister and to the silence of my mother and, finally, felt the fierce disapproval of my father. My eyes must have shown the pain in my right arm and the pain of seeing familiar faces twist to become hideous; but in his eyes, more than any of the rest of it, I'll never forget the incredible pain I saw in his eyes.

Night Diner

Last night I visited a graveyard.
Out on the old highway—
settled in the clutter of ancient tourist courts,
cluttered garages, junkyards,
and poor people—
there was a place of death.
Unlike the smooth green, summer lawns
of hillside splendor,
where, with God's sunlight and the rainbow-casting
waters of sprinklers,
the marble eternity of names and dates is preserved
for yearly flowers and yearly grief,
this was no park of maudlin verdancy
and sculptured shrubs.
Nor was it the haunted place where silent,
ghost-like breezes
chill the winter reaches of empty trees,
whisper-swirling the moon-pale markers:
no final, earthen home of the departed.

I believe her name was Karen.
Her face was neon cool,
and her eyes were some bitter, scarring secret.
Her young face was drawn rigid
by the frowning message of her lips.

"Would you care for a cup of coffee, sir?"

I looked at her, and no light shown upon me.
Such was the stark vacancy of her soul
that my mind cried out,
 "No! I don't need your coffee.
I need your smile.
I need to know your flowing breath,
your pulsing heart—

some laughing evidence of a life alive within the
night-veiled realm of your spirit."

My voice said, "Yes. Black please."

And as she filled my cup,
as she leaned close across the table
and for an instant glanced and met my gaze,
I saw the soul-sad truth of her being before me.
In the midnight clock,
in the stagger of drunks descending,
in the clutching of one more cup
against the loneliness of the night,
(there was the rattle of saucers
and the sizzle of the grill),
in the cycling of hash browns and water glasses
across the tabletops—
yes, I'm sure that "Karen" was the name
pinned to her blouse—
I saw the dreadful eyes of death.
I was drinking coffee in a graveyard of dreams.
The night paraded failure
and Karen was its child-tragic queen—
the coronated essence of its hopeless truth.

"Remember me?" he said,
and his voice was filthy,
his face a practiced smirk beneath the greasy spill
of rakish hair across his pimpled forehead.
"Sure," she said. "Would you care
for some coffee, sir?"
And to the cold hesitation of her silent stare
he only mumbled in a drunken tone,
"You don't remember me."
"I said I did," she said
and her mouth never spoke a smile
and her words never vibrated
beyond the stolid question: Coffee?
She steadily moved on up the counter
and around the tables
with the ebony lifeblood of refills,

as his smirk faded with his fantasy.

The loudmouthed braggarts were
broadcasting their losses
while the mute and humbled crusaders
of causes long deceived
stared into the steaming,
black pools of no reflection.
And all the jokes were stale
as was the heartless laughter.

It was my second refill
and I had realized her beauty.
There was grace in her movements.
Her uniform swelled
with the sensuous promise of her youth.
Her lips would have been soft in a smile.
"Karen" can be such a pretty name.
"Karen!" came the cry from the grill-lady
as artful eggs in unbroken motions
flowed from their shells.
"Order up!"

Outside, the night glowed the cadence of the stoplight
signaling the empty intersection.
I wanted to be gone
but it seemed there could be no leaving.
(And what of her father's dreams for her?
Where in the speculation
upon the playing joys of a child
could there be this night of broken drunks
and eggs over-easy?)
The dead were there,
and we, the mourners,
sat in booths and at tables and at the counter—
entrapped by the vacant telling of their deaths
in the life-void vision of their eyes.

Desperately I craved to dispel
the emptiness of her passing form,
to nourish my own being with some

glimmer of hope for her.
"Was there anything else?"
"Yes," I answered.
She waited.
"I mean no. No thank you. That's all."

In that morbid night there was no hope.
(Her name was Karen
and she was death
and she was beautiful.)
In the eyes of an old man I saw the ghosts
of a thousand perished dreams
as he slid a quarter tip across the counter
and headed back out
into the cosmic indifference of the night.

It was a graveyard of dreams
and like some thread-raveled,
patch-work quilt
I pulled my thin dreams about me,
and, yet, I felt the chill.

Her name was Karen and she was death.
And, with a crumpled dollar hastily drawn
from the pocket of my jeans,
I cast a flower upon her grave, and fled.

Philosophy

When sweet, soft pleasures
become harsh, hard memories;
and the flow of the day
is dammed to listless pools
and impotent eddies,
slowly drink an ice-chilled beer
and forget,
at least for the moment,
that God demands
rapt attention.

Travel

At first it seemed I was only fleeing confrontation with myself, but somewhere down the harried highway it was my own being I encountered ambling peacefully along, and since then I have pleasantly accepted the necessity of joining that particular manifestation of my energies that knows the heart of the gypsy.

I awoke from a cramped night in the back of my small car to the orange glow of a pre-sun morning. Emerging to stand in the gravel of a wayside rest along the two-lane west of Dumas, I perceived the etching image of distant, silhouetted farms and crucifix electric poles up the sloping curve of the earth. As I stretched beside the car and watched the work of rising light upon the horizon-bound furrows of the deep, Texas soil, I felt, in the chilled clarity of the bare breath of autumn, the open essence of vulnerable seasons and knew, by my *Rand McNally Road Atlas* and the not fully dwindled freedom of twenty-dollar bills precipitously lingering in the pockets of my jeans, that the day would possess many miles and, most significantly, that I would be the rider of those distances, and the teller of their subtle tales.

... I believe it will be Arizona this week—last month it was Minnesota, before that Virginia and somewhere, back in the wonder of timelessness, it was a low-clouded morning of mist-traveling the minor roads of the Oklahoma panhandle....

Trade-off

The eggs were undercooked,
the hash-browned potatoes white and naked,
the coffee weak,
and the little brat in the next booth aggravating.
But, oh, the waitress—
such a sweet and easy smile she had.

The Future Teller

"... and for some souls there never will be safety,"
said the soothsayer in the canvas-walled tent.
Her hand was plump and smooth as it artfully
touched the seams of my palm
(the seams of my being).
Her eyes were deep and her voice soft,
"... and for another dollar, perhaps the future
will become more clear—
perhaps there is safety in the finer lines, the subtle
lines that branch to tell the details of your life."
I said nothing.
I had no dollar to spend.
I could afford no safety.
"A woman. Yes, there might be a woman...
a dollar please,
we are so close now...."
She held my empty palm more tightly,
and she stared at me and waited.
The future cost a dollar
and I knew it to be but a gimmick,
but a dollar to tell such secrets...
"A beautiful woman or maybe great wealth,
safety in the clearing of the future—only the
shadows have been revealed.
A dollar and I can open pathways beyond any dream."
She glanced quickly out the blowing flap of the tent
and into the dusty midway night.
My hand was white where she gripped it desperately.
Her eyes darkened and,
with a pleading edge to her words, she said,
"Just one more dollar, boy,
and I can show it all to you.
Just one dollar."
And I knew the terrible
weight of that moment,

the irrational power of it.

"But I don't have a dollar," I said.
Suddenly, with broken eyes,
she dropped my damp hand
and turned away.

Clumsily, stunned by the freedom
of my unleashed palm,
I stumbled back out into the carnival lights
and the spinning thrills and the glaring madness;
and, there, just outside the canvas flap,
silhouetted by the garish night,
stood a young man with dollar bills
clasped in his anxious fist,
waiting impatiently to buy my future.

Birthday Poem—October 17, 1984

Forty years.
I don't mind the time and the loss of hair
or the gray-white patches in my beard.
I don't mind the mortality of any of this.
I don't even mind the legions
of children who are ripening
and flourishing in my wake.

What I mind about this forty-year awareness
is the recurring,
haunting sense of the desperation
of a late Sunday afternoon
that can speak so deeply
to these unfinished decades of my dreams.

The Storm

Sense the anger;
know the pain.
Loose the sorrow and
welcome the rain.

Fierce flood of the heavens,
sky-child of the sea;
drencher of drought-lands,
come rage within me.

With winds it wraps us
in the swirl of its soul.
The storm is my kinsman—
to know it, my goal.

It comes from the might
of a massive black cloud,
and with forks flashing danger
its voice is death loud.

I know that this torrent
is a part of my mind.
In the rush of its wild winds
it's myself whom I find.

Such a Generous Man

It was a cold evening a few days before Christmas. The downtown area of the city was crowded with sightseers marveling at the thousands of colored lights while frantically seeking good deals on last-minute Barbie Dolls and plastic Uzies.

I had two hours to kill while waiting for a Greyhound bus to transport me back out into the December darkness of the highway toward home. It was getting late and the swarms of strikingly beautiful women, wimpy looking men, and unruly children (i.e. yuppie families) were thinning. I skirted the epicenter of "boughs of holly" and elaborate storefront displays and wholesome consumers to wander a side street a block beyond any semblance of joy or festive light where there was not even the illusion of warmth to temper the winter's chill.

"Merry Christmas, winos," I thought without the least touch of malice or sarcasm. On some granny's cherished dish towel, it says, "Home is where the heart is," and, by damn, there is no home where there is no heart.

The thought of heading back to the neon cavern of the bus terminal was starting to sound like a pretty good idea when, from out of the darkness of an alley, a wild-eyed beggar accosted me. Thrusting himself in my path and grabbing my arm, he uttered in guttural and drunken tones, "When I have wealth, I give it away. I've been a generous man."

I instantly detested this wretched being.

We are all but one calamity away from joining the street people and, when I am able, I help with my coins and few dollars with no arrogance at the slight and temporal superiority of my economic station. That day I had already given one of my sparse dollars to a young man with a sad story and another to an old lady who was the final vestige of someone's long lost mother.

But I hated his grip on my arm and the insinuation of his words. "I've given plenty to the needy. I'm no cheap son of a bitch," he slurred. "When I've got it, I don't hold nothin' back—I've helped plenty of people with my money."

I attempted to pull away from him.

35

His grip tightened, "You think I'm a liar?!" he roared viciously with whiskey-soured breath.

"No," I said, finally shrugging myself free of the damned drunk. "I'm sure you're a very generous man."

I dug into my pocket to retrieve a quarter and buy my way clear of this philanthropist, but, instead of a quarter I grabbed a half dollar I had won by hitting "blackjack" at a dollar table back at a casino in Nevada.

"Here you are, my friend," I said with bitterness. "This is something special. I'll give you my lucky coin."

I handed him the fifty-cent piece, and he just stood there for a moment. His body jerked with drugs, his eyes were dark with the horrors of misspent spirit, his mind was a nightmare of suspicion and hatred and despicable loss. He said to me with disdain, as he turned the coin in his hand, "Screw your lucky coin, man. I'm already lucky. I ain't no cheap son of a bitch. When I help the needy, I always give a dollar."

And then with a threatening tone that sent him stumbling back toward his shadows I growled, "Well, now you're even fifty cents luckier than you were!"

And I turned and walked back toward the holy, festive lights and Barbie Doll Christmases and realized, in the blatant rage of his thanklessness, the selfishness of my gifts.

Patience and Resolution

Late winter I asked her
and she promptly said, "No."
And my footprints melted
from the sun-touched snow.

In light-leaved springtime
I risked rejection's pain,
and she just left me soaking
in the chill of drizzling rain.

And on the beach one summer night
again I begged her hand,
and with a trifling, heartless glance
she left me on the sand.

And now midst fading, golden death
of crisp, cool, shuddering fall,
though she waits 'till the Fates
tell the freeze of hell,
I'll be damned if I'll ask her at all.

Flatlands

I wonder about
these flatlands.
Towns are so insignificant
against the immensity of the land—
just forty-five-mile-per-hour speed zones,
a gas station or two, seldom a stoplight:
tree-grove outposts
adrift upon the dirt-sea wonder of the
horizon-edged Earth.
And the men who
most evenings of the turning year
drink at Harold's roadside tavern
in Cunningham, Kansas—
boisterous in this hovel of good company,
these men, these farmers—
sailors upon the soil,
tillers of the dragon-green
plows and harrows and harvesters
far out upon the swell,
where daily they are alone to know,
above the rumble and vibration
of their mighty machinery—
alone to know the voices
of untold generations of solitude.
What of these towns
and these farmers and their sky-sized fields
of cycling life?

Voices of the Hayfields

I listened to the fields today—
the fields and their conversations
with the wind.

First it was only the sound of
the wires taut in the violent gusts
sweeping before the coming clouds.
Then it settled to the steady
flow of moving airs, and I heard
the rustling of the deep green,
dense,
and spring-moist hay grass.

And later,
crossing the highway to the yellow-stark
stubble of fallow acreage,
I heard the crisp and random
whispers of the dead.

Such were the voices of the hayfields.

Biker Bar Sunday: A Family Portrait

Mountain-tall, doper-skinny;
worker-strong, Christ-faced,
martyr-cycle man
watching...
biker lady of the mountains
with her biker-baby child.

Small one with sparkling eyes dancing with the
jukebox rhythms
in infant, infinite consciousness—
mama-spun, bop to the slot-god,
shoulder-dancing baby,
spirit of the whole naive human species
reaching tiny hands for universes
in life-fresh, groping wonder.

Red-faced pretty mama,
baby wrapped about her young mind—
in reckless dance to the rock-and-roll.
Mother-free breasts and wild-flying hair,
and grin-jostled baby,
a pudgy legged necklace of life
tight about her neck.

Juggling

When she came home and tried to hide her weeping by closing the door of her room and cranking up her rock-and-roll radio, I left her alone for a while. She hadn't slammed the door. She had closed it carefully, attempting to be inconspicuous, and I knew her sadness wasn't asking for attention. It wasn't easy to stay away because the pain of a child is a miserable thing to bear from the living room as it speaks to you in fits between bedlam songs and in muffled tones through the thickness of a pillow.

When she was little, I could stop her tears with a round or two of "You Are My Sunshine" or with a popsicle or an attack of tickles. When she was little I could juggle the whole damn world dizzy in my clown-daddy hands, and it would seem we'd never have to land back in the middle of the sadness again.

Long ago when she was little.

So, I waited and suffered in the living room for a while and hoped that in the solitude of her sorrow she was learning to juggle all by herself.

It can be so lonely sometimes for a kid; for a dad.

Love: Sketch #1—Innocence

It was my sixth-grade spring and I'll tell about the delightful fragrance of Janie Meyer when love first sang its undeniable song through her young body; and how, blushing and perspiring with ancient and luring scent, it was impossible for her to hush the honesty of her fully-clothed, twelve-year-old nakedness.

Sixth grade. What a pretty young girl she was, and by the blessings of alphabetized seating my "N" was right next to her "M" there in Miss Quade's class. She laughed at my jokes, and I became silly; she loved music, and I strained my young voice to vibrate her chair with an alto that was more an atonal moan than the male mating call I had intended; her father was a preacher, and I started talking to God.

One young spring day while we struggled to complete the misshapen forms of our dreaded papier-mâché marionettes, Miss Quade, up to her old elbows in paste and newsprint, abided our laughter and chatter. I stood close to lovely Janie and said the clumsy words she heard as charming. Our arms were touching and we were giggling and covered with the pasty goo of our creations and her lips parted as if to speak yet there was no sound. There was only the sweet smell of uninhibited, innocent lust in the singing of her body to my heart.

Oh, the aroma of love.

Love: Sketch #2—A Seasoning of Lust

The night when I was a seventeen-year-old boy and Coney Island became much more than a hot dog; naive dreams, yet alive in sensations of fear and lust and hope, rode the night-sky Ferris wheel high above the mobs and shrieking thrills of the midway.

Elizabeth was her pretty name and she clung so tightly to me and in the hovering moment at the pinnacle of the great wheel's rotation, when the entire night, with its carnival blur of tin-speaker sounds and mingling popcorn/cotton candy smells and kaleidoscope visions of light and motion, was rocking dangerously beneath us; Elizabeth, with her long brown hair spilling down across her shoulders and the wild brilliance of her eyes flashing the excitement of this infinite instant of my young life, whispered, her soft lips and the warmth of her breath brushing my ear as she spoke, "Take me down to the beach."

Love: Sketch #3—The Real Thing

You sat so comfortably upon my lap. You kissed me and I was wild.

What days we were having when suddenly I found I could say "I love you" with such corny truth as any old song had ever sung.

And you sat upon my lap there in the living room of your small apartment and I said to you, "You know you've got to marry me, don't you?"

And, of course, you knew it.

And, by God, of course, you did.

Love: Sketch #4—Carnal Bitterness

It was some summer night cast to the swirl of loss and emptiness. Her name might have been Tricia and we drank a beer at some roadside pizza place and later that night we screwed in a grassy field near Lorton until the cops ran us off and we finished our banging standing up with her pinned against the door of her sports car.

Later, she told me I was a better than average lover, and I said something about her tits. She was the first "one night stand" of my new single life, and it seemed to take an inordinate amount of grunting, groaning, and lying to finish the deed.

Ah, love.

Love: Sketch #5—My Loving Friend

My beloved friend, though I give you the subtle, flaming harmonies of my love, the paramour that is this blessed and cursed art of mine gives you due cause for jealousy. My truest infidelity is of the soul— long taken by the lust and lure of the Wind: My soul that clasps to you while reaching for the deadly exhilarating caress of the Gods.

Hold fast, my love; the tempest is so strong.

Space and Destiny

My nephew,
Eddie is his name,
tried to start junior college
but he couldn't find a parking space
so he said to hell with "higher" education.

Now he's an artist.

Night Walker

Autumn is damp and chilled.
The yellow-orange leaves lie flat upon the sidewalk.
I walk upon them and they are somber
in the gray air's shift toward darkness.
Draped windows glow in the illusion of warmth.
The heavy air smells of fireplace smoke.
It is a street of old trees and close houses
shuddering in the chill of damp autumn's evening.
As I pass with slow cadenced step,
I know that brick and flame and light
are not sufficient to dissuade the message
of the flat fallen leaves and drizzling air.
In gray and pastel shades, houses hover upon
the edge of my passing.
Silhouetted tree limbs grope the dimming sky.

Out of the death-whispering dusk!
Into the tavern's blessed, gaudy warmth
and cacophonous laughter,
with soaked coat cast aside and burning brandy
sipped and descending the chilled reaches of the body—
a sandwich with plenty of grilled onions
and grease-hot fries,
and, of course, a deep and friendly draught of beer.
And, yes, my friends, we will smile a bit
on this night of the moribund season.
We'll have no cares of dying leaves and dying heat
and shifting season's shortening days.
We're a hearty bunch and the beer will flow
and night will stay at bay awhile.
Roll the dice for the jukebox coins!
(A waitress is a pretty thing to tease your tortured mind
and sift and drift away in a folding waltz for a dollar tip.)
Rack them up! I'll break them with the voice of a whip.

I'll scatter the rainbow balls to the corners
of the green-felt earth,
and then,
with the delicate precision of a blues singer's softest tones,
I'll make the cue ball a shadow-deft brother
of the Grim Reaper. Watch them; hear them fall.
And where did she go, my stealthy lass?
We'll be needing another round.
I'll buy us another beer's worth of time.
(My friends have first names only,
and I only find them here—within this shallow harbor
of the vast and violent sea of black night.)
Cards are shuffled, dealt, and spent;
songs are played, and played again;
old jokes told and richly re-laughed,
politicians cursed, battles brandished, secrets lost,
promises broken, lies forgiven,
holy good-intentions spoken—
and all as harmless as a flame.

Someone says, "It's getting late."

Returned into the autumn night,
stunned by the trauma of much-damned time
and its irreparable spending of life's moments,
I know again that it is a cold truth
to be a wanderer of the empty streets that stretch long
beside the fortresses of warmth and sleep.
The houses are dark.
And within them are sleepers with minds escaped
to distant dreams,
wrapped warm in thick blankets,
night flesh convoluted
within slumbering night flesh
against the sound
of solitary footfalls in staccato movement
through street-lit patterns.
Sometimes I am the sound;
sometimes I am the echo of the sound.
My shoes are voices of the pavement—
spoken to the wet night sky and to the reverberating

stone of the city.

Autumn night is chilling gloom
and leaves expended upon the ground,
a deep and dampening mist,
and a soul that walks alone.

The Persistence of a Haunting Truth

And so,
in avoidance of rainbows and other illusions,
he would have shut down the eyes
and heart and listening senses so brutally touched
and seemingly only blessed
by devils and holyangels of deception
and their much cursed fascination;
and,
with curtailed lust,
would have settled to while the ending days of decades
unmemorable away in the silence of fear-muted apathy,
but for the inexplicable persistence
of waking dreams and sleepless nights
ever mumbling
in ceaseless and immortal tongues
of toilsweat and tearsalt and damnedlove.

Club Earth

So, if indeed *They* have sent me to this planet to have a good time (a thought this afternoon—that, as some sort of Cosmic R&R, I was deposited in this world to wander among the natives, drink a few beers, and then return to the more purposeful toil of tilling the Infinite), then why have I allowed myself to be infected by the local viruses of guilt and conscience?

Like the infamous Montezuma's Revenge of Mexico, this land's equally distressing John Calvin's Revenge haunts my vacation in this region of self-despising, Protestant Christians.

Compassion, honest love, and other gifts of the soul are no problem. Such notions are as much a part of the Universe as they are of Denver, Colorado, and other points local and Earth-bound. I am, regardless of Cosmic coordinates and mandates of the Wind, a spirit of love.

Why, then, do such pangs of guilt and regret haunt the best efforts I am capable of giving this respite from Eternity?

God knows when I'll ever have another vacation.

"Barkeep, another round please, and, perhaps, some of those beer nuts. I'll match you for the jukebox. Aren't there ever any women in this place?"

Smallchild #1

When the smallchild opened the classroom door and collected the attendance slip, I felt such sadness. The smallchild was short so he had to stretch to reach the hook that held the slip, and he made an audible sound in his grasp—some combination of clumsy feet against the door and a faint gasp of air.

My class of perfect fullchildren turned to witness the spectacle of the smallchild who had invaded their fullchild world. I don't hate the fullchildren for their ignorance, but I do hate their ignorance. I detest the humor of permanent misfortune, the retard-cripple kind of "hey, look at the freak" joke at the expense of God's smallchild victims of His capital "C," Cosmic level cruelties.

The smallchild took the attendance slip and stumble-closed the door behind him to the mumbled gaiety of the fullchildren's naively vicious notion of amusement.

I needed to cry out to the world, to the Gods, to the pitiless imperfection of Nature. But what cry could ever reach the solitude of the smallchild as he made his zig-zag rounds down the empty school hall with its burlesque stage doors and alpine attendance slips?

A Gift from My Mother

My mother would laugh and cry at the same time when she watched me drunkenly walk up the long hill to the house after an evening's intemperance in the city. It was years later before she told me. For years I never knew that she was watching. Waiting up for my return.

Silence was her gift to me. I had thought I was alone in my ruin.

I was years past my youth before she told me the feelings she had known as she witnessed her twenty-year-old boy crashing face first through neighborhood hedges with swagger deteriorating to stumble, to fall. All her life she sensed with her heart, and her heart would break at the sight of my misspent energies, slap-sticking home in the gray of her long night's vigil into dawn. She couldn't help but laugh, though, at the antics of her baby boy—little Robert almost a man and still a toddling child. She would cry and laugh silently at a darkened upstairs window, she later told me, as she loved her clown-boy struggling up the long hill toward home.

Bless her. She never told me then.

* * * *

There was the all day and all night bout with the twenty-nine beers and the Inauguration Day Parade, 1965. Lyndon Baines Johnson was hot for a full term of military and social mayhem. I fought the crowd sufficiently to see the President's huge left ear pass by in a motorcade and said to hell with it and headed out Pennsylvania Avenue to Brownley's Bar and Grill. Brownley's had mugs of Ballantine beer for a quarter, and part of the parade would pass right in front of the place.

I started early that afternoon. Twenty years old and who could tell what snares to the wildness might await my coming days. It was time to drink. Life that young day was not to be weighed or measured.

Afternoon beer. I sat at a front table by the window and watched as low-licensed limousines and teams of precision drill Eskimos passed by. There were horses and motorcycles and soldiers and marching bands. There was so much beer that day. I sat there for hours writing letters of love, poems of sorrow, and essays of outrage while the parade thinned and finally fizzled to a few straggling drummers and heaps of horseshit scattered across the wide pavement.

So, on through the evening, I drank the cheap brew until closing at two and then staggered back downtown to the Greyhound Bus Terminal to catch a local run south to the far suburbs and home.

Twenty-nine beers. Jesus.

I didn't start throwing up until the twenty blocks had passed and I was shivering out in front of the bus terminal. Washington is a cold son of a bitch in the wintertime, and I was hanging on to a "No Parking" sign and heaving youth upon the hard pavement of New York Avenue with taxi cabs and prostitutes and drug dealers and wind-lost travelers of the long night swimming around the periphery of my blurred consciousness.

"Hey, man, you're looking bad. You need a friend." I tried to straighten up. His arm was around me and I could smell his sour breath.

"I can help you. I can make you feel good."

I shrugged my shoulders, but he held tight.

"I'll be your friend. Come with me, child-man. I've got a nice place for you."

It's been well over twenty years now, and, yet, the image is so clear. His paled lips moving so close to my face; the sickening, sweet smell of his perfume; the feel of his hands gripping me as he pulled me toward some shadowy edge beyond the street.

"I'll be so good for you, sick one. I can make you well," he breathed with devil-lisping, serpent's voice.

Then there was the shattered look upon his chiseled face as he hovered, suspended momentarily—stunned, frozen there where I had smashed him violently against the brick wall. Was he laughing or crying as he shrieked past me and disappeared into the city night?

Of course, for all I knew, I was alone. The Richmond Bus would be loading at Gate 3 in about an hour, and twenty broken miles to Woodbridge would mean some sleep.

I was feeling a respite from nausea. I was never afraid. I was profoundly empty though—more empty than I had ever known throughout the entire odyssey of my childhood. The ancient, simple

55

times of simple knowledge. The first day of school times—first day, first kiss, last class, last glance down the winter night-street moments of my ever departing childhood.

The terminal smelled of neon-lighted death, so I wandered over to 11th Street and sprawled down the steps of a stairwell leading to a darkened basement shop. I leaned back against the filthy cement and waited. The dizziness returned, the sickness of too damned much beer and too damned much loss. I curled up like a fetus, my face even with the sidewalk, my writhing body contorted by the contractions of the birth into a timeless light, less forgiving than that of the youth from which I had just been severed.

A dignified looking old couple, probably a diplomat and his wife, left a restaurant up the street and walked by. He saw me first and directed his lady to the far side of the sidewalk in avoidance of my spectacle. They looked down at me with such disgust. It was as if I were some rodent crouching in a sewer.

I looked straight out at their feet and then up at their faces and then, in a shaken yet boisterous voice, I shouted them out of the nightmare of that wretched hour with the fine old phrase, "How low can he go!?"

I thought I was alone in that stairwell. Just myself and the reverberating sound of my shivering laughter.

* * * *

How was I to know she waited up for me, twenty miles and an epoch away, in a room lit only by the glow of the tip of her cigarette and the blue light spilling in from the empty street?

Such a gift, her silence. Such a gift to spare me the guilt.

My Mother's Fried Eggs

My mother's fried eggs were seldom right—
somehow spoiled by broken yellows or burnt whites;
gaggingly under-done to spill amoeba-like
across my early morning plate,
to make limp the once crisp edges of my toast,
or leatherly overcooked—suitable for shoe soles
or tiny catcher's mitts.

But always—throughout the odyssey of my life in her home,
from infancy's cheerful and cherished ingestion
of any spoon-fed goo playfully pressed to my lips
to the final stages of my impatient, yet hesitant youth
when hangovers and restlessness precluded
even a hint of an appetite—
always my mother's fried eggs were conceptually cooked
to artful, loving perfection
upon the heart-heated stove of her eternal kitchen.

The Insensitive Man

It had been coming for years, the cloudiness. It wasn't until the kitchen fires that my father had to acknowledge the existence of a problem with Mom. Until then, in his strong and firm manner, he had shown no outward recognition of the fact that she was losing track of things. He has always believed in ignoring, as long as possible, matters about which he has no control. At times, those of us who love him have thought him to be insensitive to some of the dilemmas of our lives. It has turned out, however, that early on, he realized he wasn't God and, hence, couldn't cure all of the ills afflicting either the world or his own family and chose not to waste his mortally limited energies doing battle with impossibility.

But then the cooking oil would be forgotten on the electric burner and the kitchen walls would have to be repainted; and eventually he would have to cook for himself and for the lady who had prepared his meals for over forty years. It had started with momentary lapses of memory and then progressed over the short span of a few years to only occasional moments of clarity.

Senility he couldn't fix; helplessness he could work on. For months leading to years he expended his physical and emotional being in the constant care of his mate.

This insensitive man.

And by the final weeks, when her wonderful mind had gone from being partly cloudy to having the steel-smooth cast of a winter's day, and even her own childhood, her own history, had retreated to inaccessible realms of her fading memory; when even "now" had ceased to have focus—when all who loved her knew death was the only kindness left for her; he, too, had nearly wasted away in the struggle for the last days of her life and dignity.

My robust father was bone-thin and his voice was a near-empty vessel by the time Mom died.

And so it was that this insensitive man taught me such a lesson in love.

**Lines Written in Defiance
of Metaphoric Seasons and Suns**
(In defense of a twelve-month,
twenty-four hour existence past forty)

Autumn is no dusk,
nor is spring the morn.
Each season's unfolding
is an entity born.

I am no watcher of late afternoon.
Today is the sunrise,
the sunset, the moon.

Encounter

His eyes were dark and fast. His lashes were long and graceful. He had the dark hair of his race: *la raza*. His arms were wire and his hands tight. Nine years old and he crouched in the tree like a beast.

He could hear the sound of his name calling through the park, and occasionally he caught a glimpse of the frantic searchers as they dashed about the bushes and ponds and turning lanes, shouting his name as they ran.

"Paul. Paul. Come back, Paul. You can have cake and Kool-Aid, Paul. Where are you?"

He knew the words. He knew them well. He was Paul, and sometimes it was a good name as in "Paul, you got it right, you're a good boy, Paul!" And sometimes it was harsh like "Paul! Don't pinch. Sit down. Sit down, Paul! Don't pinch!" And cake was sweet and sticky between the fingers and on the face and forehead and all along the tracks of his ever-stretching hands. And he knew the sound of a love-spoken voice and the feel of love-burnt tears smashed tightly against the tenseness of his face.

But better than all of these things—even better than he knew the nervous Kool-Aid that would leap in splashes from the brittle picnic cups and spill cool into his throat—better than the sad, long looks of his mother, better than all of these things he knew the good feel of the tree.

The tree with its rough smudging bark against his now bare feet. The moving, swaying, gentle tree that drew him higher and higher. The solid roughness of the tree against his enwrapping arms. The tree to which he clung high above the calling park.

He hung tightly to the trunk and limbs like a koala.

* * * *

Ed Morris had been a photographer for too many years. He would think back over the eons to his youth and laugh a quiet, cynically embarrassed laugh in little air whiffs through his nose when he recalled the idealism of a young man with a camera and a world full of shape and balance and texture. He would think of what a fool he had been and about how abruptly it had been necessary for him to learn where a man could make a living with images. He had learned about economics early into the first baby, and, by the time he was well into the second, he had almost eliminated the surges of regret and remorse at the thought of his aborted dreams.

His sign read:
The Morris Studio
Family Portraits
Weddings

* * * *

When a child is lost and the streets are busy with terrible cars and trucks and buses, a mother feels terror and darts about frantically sobbing at her imagined discoveries. She asks them all, "Have you seen him? He was wearing a red shirt. Have you seen my little boy?" But not Mrs. Diaz. Her eyes were dull; her actions sluggish. They had called her to come to the park with words she knew would always come. "Paul has run away. We can't find him. We're sorry."

He always ran away. Even in his empty bedroom with the door closed and locked, he ran away with his hands slapping and scratching at the paneled walls and with his screams muffled within his tightly closed lips.

At the special school they told her, "Paul is doing so much better this year. He understands us when we speak. Sometimes he obeys." And she had thought, "Yes, he runs faster, he climbs quicker, he is harder to catch now."

Mrs. Diaz had been a lovely woman. Her rare smiles were flashes from a distant and hazy, but magnificent sensuality. The contours of her body were veiled and dulled by a thickness. She was a woman of tragically hopeless beauty. She had become numb and unmoving and impassive as if the contours of her mind were also dulled by a thickness.

And from limb to limb he could crawl—the little boy with dark hair and the stains of a picnic upon his tight face. He never smiled.

* * * *

"You kids had better smile today when the man takes the picture. This is costing me a damn fortune."

(Family Portraits)

61

Sometimes it is a woman's way to win an argument by gradually eroding the resistance of her adversary. This had been the case with Mrs. Murphy and the family portrait. It had taken her over a year to bitch and prod and maneuver her husband into agreeing to hire Mr. Morris to take one of his very expensive family portraits and she was quite proud of herself in winning the long battle.

"Hurry, children," she said, "Mr. Morris is a busy man and can only spare us a few minutes."

"All that money for a few damn minutes," muttered Mr. Murphy as he straightened his wide tie and searched out the reflection of his large, heavy face for correctable flaws.

The children were in their best clothes. Clothes that were purchased by Mrs. Murphy for very special and very uncomfortable occasions.

"Don't complain, Harold," she told her husband. "Mr. Morris is a famous photographer in this town—and so creative. We were lucky to get him at all and much less at such a reasonable price." She was wallowing in her victory and he knew it and, also, he knew there was nothing he could do about it at that point. He had lost. He had to shut up.

The two little boys were dressed in sport coats and wore little bow ties and little vests. Mr. Murphy had a huge vest that perfectly matched his straining suit. The little girl wore a pink dress that scratched and ruffled around her small legs.

The children stood stiffly by the car in their fine clothes with Mrs. Murphy and her rare pearls while Mr. Murphy gruffly locked the front door and then reluctantly shuffled toward them.

If a neighbor had been watching, she would have sworn the Murphys were going to a funeral.

* * * *

The once beautiful, now tired Mrs. Diaz wandered slowly and quietly around the large park as the frenzied searchers ran and cried out for her son.

"I'm so sorry," the teacher had told her. "We had finished with the food and were all sitting in a circle singing songs and Paul just disappeared. Usually someone stays with him, but—it couldn't have been more than a minute—my aide left him so she could laugh at the songs with the rest of us, and he was gone. I'm sorry."

Mrs. Diaz had assured the teacher and the aide it couldn't be helped and that Paul had been running away for as long as he had been able to run.

And she watched the other children in a close bunch by the picnic table. They were misfits by the standards of the world. They were developmentally delayed, crippled, twisted little children clumped together in a minute corner of a huge green park. She watched the little crippled girl with sparkling eyes laugh at the tickling of the small boy with no hair or real words and she thought how fortunate their mothers were to have such perfect children.

Paul was a thin, tense muscle who spoke to no one and looked at no one.

* * * *

"What a fine looking family you are!"

"Thank you, Mr. Murphy. You're so kind."

They were on the sidewalk in front of the Morris Studio. He had met them there to suggest a highly creative alternative to the standard studio portrait.

"Why don't we all walk a few blocks to the park and take the photos there. It's so much more natural that way. I know a huge old tree that will make a marvelous background for your photograph."

And for the twentieth time that spring Ed Morris marched a family troupe down to the park he used for a stage and toward the tree he used as a prop.

Mr. Murphy had a great jolly mustache which clashed bitterly with his hard, cruel eyes. Mrs. Murphy had a double chin that lapped beneath her sarcastic lips. The boys were mean and had flat noses, and the precious little girl had teeth that were much too large for her thin, little mouth.

"There's the tree over there," said Mr. Morris. "Isn't it a fine old tree?"

"What a lovely tree," said Mrs. Murphy.

* * * *

And high above with a nerve-thin body paced Paul between the forked limbs.

* * * *

"Here we go. Let's see. You stand in the middle, Mr. Murphy, with Mrs. Murphy beside you. Children you can be in front here.

Let's put this pretty little girl in the middle. There, that's good—right in front of this fine old tree. This won't take long at all. That's right, Mr. Murphy, Mrs. Murphy. Close it up a bit."

With the camera set, Ed Morris looked through the square view-finder at the inverted image of five, forced smiles. Mr. Murphy's great, wide, bitter smile; Mrs. Murphy's smile of feigned adoration and warmth; the boys' demonic little crooked smiles; and the little girl's teeth. He saw them all huddled together there at the foot of the great, natural tree with their smiles and their ties, and their starched ruffles and perfect pearls.

* * * *

"There he is! There he is!" shouted a searcher. "There. I can see his red shirt high up in that old tree. Mrs. Diaz, we've found Paul!"

And Mrs. Diaz could see her boy, and she walked slowly toward the massive, old tree with no sound and no expression on her face.

"Mommy, there's a boy in the tree."

"Shut up," snapped Mr. Murphy. "Let's get this over with."

"That's it. That's it," sang Mr. Morris. "Everyone smile."

What's in a Name?

Down at Reese's Cafe on South Broadway
at two-thirty in the morning
my eggs were a little cold when I got them
because the cook called them ready with,
"Links and easies up, Queen Bee!"
Her name was Gloria and she was guarding
all that hadn't been lost to her
in the all-night place.
"My name isn't Queen Bee, you asshole!"
she shouted.
"My name is Gloria."
And they bickered life and death
while my links and easies waited
until at last Gloria had her name
and she slid the plate
down the counter to me
with a wink and a bottle of Tabasco.

I didn't mind—
a little cold, but so tasty.

North Temple Street

It's sad, I guess—
the railroad bums
and the scraps of litter that
toss about their feet
as they congregate around the dumpster
behind the DAV Thrift Store—
because it is autumn in the heartless town
and the reward for submission to Mission's prayer
is as bland as its watery soup and egg-salad sandwiches.

While pulling the insufficiency
of the layered tatter of his surplus shirts
about him,
one of the alley-huddled ménage said,
as he studied the cluttered pavement
and contemplated the deepening chill
of the coming darkness,

"So, what do we do now?"

Communication

At least we're laughing.
Though we are often choked with fear and hatred,
at least together we can laugh at the shallow singing
of a dim and daily joke:
we old fools and communists.

The Street Beggar's Story

It was a four-bar night
in a mountain town.
I was stumbling and falling
on the frozen ground.
(You don't know what you've lost
until you see just what you've found.)
And the howling winter nights were just beginning.

I started out strong,
and I started out bold;
I ended up bleeding in the
ice-snow cold.
(The world is staying younger—
it's only me who's getting old.)
And in the winter wind my mind was thinning.

Near sobered by my shivers,
I got back upon my feet.
In the tavern there was laughter,
but whiskey fools you with its heat,
so I walked on toward the darkness
with my evening incomplete.
While the winter kept closing up the sky.

In the Colorado Rockies
on a beaten barroom night,
I had felt the rages rising
but I'd left before the fight.
Sometimes you know that leaving
is the only move that's right.
And in the winter's wind a man could die.

It was half way up an alley
near an old and rusted truck,

when whiskey legs and half-drunk kegs
had turned upon my luck.
I slipped and stalled and soundly sprawled
and deep in snow was stuck.
There's no relenting to the blowing winter wind.

I was fallen and freezing and sorely tired
and in a drunken downcast heap,
with too many years of losing
and too few hopes to reap.
It was strange right there in that freezing air
but it seemed like a fine time to sleep.
And the winter's death-grip cold became a friend.

While the blizzard began, by an old trash can
I was drifting toward my reward.
In delirium's dreams, life's not what it seems,
and in wild and good times my mind soared,
as about me
the snowy winds roared.
And the clouds of the storm dropped down.

Her name was Sally and her eyes were blue
and her lips were soft and sweet.
Her heart was loving and her touch like fire
as she drew me so close to her heat.
(It's sad sometimes that it's only in dreams
where true love we chance to meet.)
And the frigid winter snow filled the town.

There were beaches and sunshine, waves coming in
and an afternoon drink in the shade;
laughter and music and women and lust
and a feeling that never could fade.
(What a world of pleasure
with my dreams I had made.)
While the blowing cold snow piled up deep.

There were people long past me or just cast aside
whose faces I clearly did see,
and feelings of love and acceptance

long lost by the old form of me.
(Too gruff and rough and lonesome
for the pleasure of good company.)
While beneath the white snow I did sleep.

I stirred for a moment
from my fantasized bliss,
and felt on my face
the snow's cold deadly kiss,
and laughed from the snow bank,
"What the hell will I miss!"
And the dreams and the winds swirled away.

They say they found me all frozen and stiff,
in the sunlight of the early next day.
They say that they figured me dead for sure
'till they heard my grizzled face say,
"Can't you see you're keepin' a man from his sleepin',
now get the hell out of my way."
But the storm nor the dreams were to stay.

* * * *

They sent me to Denver way down on the plains
where the room and the treatment were free,
and with me poor and tattered, to them nothing mattered
so they cut off my left leg at the knee.
Now that was the reason that spring was the season
before they turned me back free.
And the theft of my winter was a terrible crime.

Now, instead of a leg, I walk on a peg
with a crutch I made from a stick.
And in place of my hills, I've got pain that near kills
and begging for coins is my trick.
In downtown doorways in the sad part of town,
I drink wine 'till I'm passed out or sick.
And the winter had passed in its time.

My boozing buddies are Tim and Mike
and a gruesome threesome we are.
We beg and we steal and we trade and we deal

and then we head down for the bar.
With Tim and his palsy and Mike raving mad,
it's good that it's not very far.
The snow's mostly melted; the peaks are all brown.

But, I've noticed of late from my bed on the streets,
there's a definite chill in the air.
Curled up in a corner awaiting the dawn
from beneath my blanket I stare.
I look toward the mountains and their barren peaks,
and I think of what waits for me there.
And autumn's chilled fingers can reach to the ground.

My buddies have been here for lifetimes of grief
for more years than they'd dare to tell.
I've been limping these sidewalks for over six months,
and I know I can't stay in this hell.
Mike and his sobbing and Tim with his shakes—
it's a place where no soul can get well.
And the cycle of seasons is turning toward cold.

It's a coin I'll be bumming or maybe a buck,
I've tried to cut back on my booze.
And soon out of this cage, this spirit will rage
from this land where even dreams lose.
(Sleep's not so fine when you're dead from the wine
and someone can be stealing your shoes.)
And blankets of snow on the mountains unfold.

It won't be too long now when a deep bank of snow
will find my body again,
and I'll drink a toast to a thousand hells
and to winter, my very best friend.
And return to my dreams, my beautiful dreams
and stay with them to the end.
And winter, at last, is nearly in range.

I'll say farewell to Denver,
farewell to the street.
So long to the sidewalks
and the mission's cursed heat.

I'll bum my bus fare
from all who I meet.
Do you suppose you could spare me some change?

The Ages

The other day I was sitting in a tavern
in a small town out on the Oregon coast
when Socrates, who was sitting up the bar from me
looking out the window,
yelled to Jesus, who was sitting down the bar from me,
"Jesus! The wind is blowing so hard the sea gulls
have to walk!"
And there we were:
Socrates and Jesus,
and Buddha back in a booth with Madam Curie
and Willie Mays—
all of us just sitting there
laughing our asses off.

Arrogance and Apathy
The State of Art

Artists should be leaders of a culture—not its pampered, eccentric parasites. There is a much-neglected responsibility on the part of those blessed with creative gifts and energies to communicate with the masses.

As, conversely, there is a much-neglected responsibility on the part of the masses to demand such attention of its artists.

The art of this country should be an extension of the democratic principles that supposedly govern it. In the creation of the aesthetic expression of our culture, Denison, Iowa, and Stuart, Virginia, and Yachats, Oregon, should be as integral as New York and San Francisco.

Denison should be a part of the artist's vision of America.

But what of the hundreds of New York galleries and the scores of huge publishing houses? What of the world-renowned symphonies? The self-proclaimed connoisseurs might ask: What does the Denison Community Band and Orchestra really know of Philip Glass? (Om-pah-pah, om-pah-pah and a medley of the greatest show tunes of Rogers and Hammerstein, the marches of John Phillip Sousa —how about that "Stars and Stripes Forever?")

What do these bumpkins, so far from the modern art scene, have to do with the cutting edge of *avant garde* culture? Well, I might ask: What do the purveyors of this modern scene—those who arrogantly fling the oil, who cryptically quote the egocentric patter, who dissonantly contort the tones and rhythms of the human song— what do the painters and the poets and the composers who are schooled and patronized in the folly of such conceit that they believe their whims and personal miseries need not touch the elusive and powerful Universals to be art? What do the contemporary "masters" know of Denison, Iowa?

And, of course: How much of a damn does Denison give anyway?

I was drinking beer at the Oasis Bar in that very town not long ago. The lady sitting around the corner of the bar from me said, "So, what kind of books do you write?" I told her I was working on a book of poetry, and all she said, before turning her attention back down the bar to a man whose fascinating life's work had something to do with rendering dead animals into dog food, was "Oh. You must really be smart."

Well, it turns out, my lady (Hey, maybe if you talk real sweet with him, someday he'll give you a ride in his big truck with the high wooden sides and the hoofed legs sticking up like drought-killed trees), that you're wrong. I'm not very smart at all. I'm not smart enough to understand the majority of the poetry printed in the *New Yorker Magazine* or in poetry journals stacked in dusty abandon upon shelves of university libraries. The poets they publish usually leave me short of knowing what they're talking about. They make me feel like someone who is purposefully being excluded from an insider's conversation. And when I do muster sufficient cerebral oomph to grasp the chosen words, hell, I'm not smart enough to understand why anyone would want to publish another of ten thousand complex and highly introspective variations on the theme: Woe is me, life sucks.

The fact is, pretty lady of Denison, it wasn't my fuzzy beard or my thinning locks or the fact that I might have belched into my beer a time or two that sent you running to that lackluster, agrarian grim reaper down the bar—the truth is, just the mention of my art intimidated you.

So much, in fact, America, that we have, for the most part, allowed ourselves to be excluded from access to the expressions of the richest talents of our culture.

Somewhere along the line back in the twenties or so, someone decided, "We artists don't have to talk to those turkeys. Let them have their moving pictures and radio shows—let's just talk to ourselves and ignore the dullard mass."

And, obviously, we of the dullard masses went right along with the plan and, over the decades, have evolved a popular culture that drums and ho-hums and lightly amuses and sedates the emptiness of our hours rather than stimulating the perceptive and creative gifts of our amazing minds and spirits.

I taught English in secondary schools for years; I have written poetry as a calling and as a life's precious endeavor for over three decades; I have broached the subject of these special utterances in countless conversations across the full expanse of this nation and, with few exceptions, the poetry of our age of American literature has made most of us feel too stupid to understand it.

"I don't get that shit," says America of its poems and paintings and symphonies.

And the tragedy is: "I don't give a shit if you get it or not," says Art.

Why is it tragic that Art has abandoned the common people in order to dwell in minute cloisters of self-gratification, wearing values bought right off the rack with the rest of "the emperor's new clothes?"

What's the big deal? So art entrepreneurs plaster the walls of galleries and art museums with shapes and shadows of exaggerated ego, and poets rewrite the scripts of their own nightmares, and symphonies trash their Stradivari for roasting pans percussed by soup ladles—what difference does it make if Denison, Iowa, doesn't get it?

It is tragic because, when Twentieth Century art was allowed to stray from the realm of the people, the people compromised the power of the human spirit and settled for so much less. "At least when I'm watchin' TV it don't make me feel stupid. At least I can get it."

We "get it" and we "get it" immediately. It's all there for us to absorb with such minimal effort or involvement or thought. And the more we acquiesce to such pap, the weaker we become. While the artists are off in some secluded loft playing with themselves, the nation settles in for another evening of situation comedies and good-guy-bad-guy violence. "Can somebody get me another beer?" says America.

Excluded from the challenge and intensity of great art, the masses have lost the deeper soundings of the human spirit.

This is half the tragedy.

The other half: Art, estranged from the needs and truths of the common people, has lost its soul.

We are in this together, we poets and we peasants.

When, as has been the trend in this century, Art attempts to distance itself from those it is meant to encounter, such vanity, such disdain for the real world, violates its most precious purpose: to communicate, and by doing so, to inspire.

Artists should proudly lead the aesthetic and spiritual endeavors of a culture. However, in these modern times, this has rarely been the case. We live in an apathetic era of the arts—with artists too removed from the masses to touch, and the masses too lazy to reach.

Labor

Winds of the Cosmic howl and touch my times upon Earth, and they batter me and caress me with terror and beauty.

I play banjo to my sunshine hillsides and bow to the applause of wind-rustling pine boughs.

I delight in the myriad stars of the wild-darkness of mountain night though they have given me no more answers than have preachers, or philosophers, or beer.

I am a poet as is the river the voice of fallen rain.

When I sing the songs of humanity, they are the bellow of a bawdy beast, the whisper of a subtle lover, the cry of flesh lost to the labyrinth of mortality, the anthem of a soul as small as an alpine flower and as vast as Eternity.

It is a wonder to be alive for the lifelong trauma of my birth.

Cold Compassion
A Modern Tale of Love and War

I

In the apartment next door,
just the other side of the paper-thin, word-thin wall,
there was a war going on,
but we were blissfully lost in the ever turning rapture
of love upon the humps and heaves of our hide-a-bed.

In the apartment next door,
just four steps up the dimly lit hallway
to a door marked HELL,
there was a famine going on,
but it had none of our concern, for our mouths were aflame
and ever gorged in suckling consumption
of the manna of lusting love.

In the apartment next door,
back to back with our toilet
and with mutually vulnerable hot and cold water pipes,
there was ever the cry of the lonely,
but it didn't matter to us.
Our hearts were ever tethered
by the tangling of our limbs and loins
and sweat-matted love hair.

Oh, yes, of course there was noise.
Isn't there always noise in a low rent apartment?
(Sometimes when the war was at its ferocious worst,
and we could distinguish, oh how clearly we could
sometimes distinguish the cries
of one death from the others,
we would have to smother ourselves in pillows
and air-gasped love whispers
licked wetly into

each other's goose-bump waiting ears.)
Sometimes,
yes
sometimes, when the children would cry
(not really so loudly—too weak to be loud—
more shrill than loud)
sometimes we would have to growl and squeal and rip
each other's willing skin with love-teeth
until the love-pain would make us wail
in piercing screams of ecstasy to drown them out.
And
when the lonely would whisper wall-told words
like
"I'm falling, I'm falling,
God, help me, where am I,
I'm falling,"
when the lonely would tap upon the paper-thin wall
and wait in long,
ever-long moments for us to answer,
well,
truthfully,
sometimes we would just have to snug
our momentarily satiated bodies
into cute little interwoven leg shelves
and arm notches
and...
and sleep.

II

I don't think it had to happen.
It wasn't inevitable.
But it did.
Surely, it didn't matter anyway.
But it did happen.
One night,
oh, what a night of giving and sharing
and touching and loving it had been,
one night the roaring war and the whining hunger
and the sobbing solitude
upon an instant

ceased.
It became quiet in the apartment next door.
Stunned by the clear sound
of our own hearts beating
in the matrix of the curtain-like quiet;
startled by the blade-sharp,
lightning-sudden silence,
we turned our love-glowing awareness
from the realms of each other's
pool-like eyes
and knew for a moment the empty darkness about us.
Then,
with a terrible crash our door burst open,
and the hordes
from the apartment next door rushed in—
such a flood of arms and armor
and skull-faced babies
and soul-less eyes—
and they were upon us
and all the unrelenting ages of noise next door
had been given hands,
and all the hands were upon our bodies
and we were held tightly to the sheets of our bed.
And then it became silent again.
So many hands held us, so many eyes watched,
but only three took action.

The soldier, with scars and gaping wounds
and filth-splattered face and fever-scorched eyes,
with an artful flick of his bayonet and barely
a touch of pain, marched back out into dim hallway
with my masculinity dangling from its tip
like an old money pouch sagging with heavy coin.

The shaking, bowlegged child,
a tiny fork in one hand,
a razor-sharp steak knife in the other,
how like a surgeon he deftly touched
my lady's pleasure and then,
with it hooked between his sparse, soft
teeth like the succulent heart of a grape,

wobbled through the door
and away.
And the lost lady with her hair pulled sadly
across her face like a shawl—
leaving only the mad depth of her eyes,
how she laid upon our watching faces
her cold hands and withdrew from us
our minds and souls,
and then wrapped them around her like a quilt
and drifted out the door.
In silence, they all followed and were gone.
We didn't move until we heard
the slamming of their door
and the return of the noise.

III

It didn't matter.
It wasn't such a great time,
but it didn't matter.
I'm sure of that;
for,
just as soon as we were certain they had devoured
us only as a respite from their war and their hunger
and their loneliness,
just as soon as we were sure they were
fully engulfed in the raging of wall sounds,
we got up and secured the door
(stronger than ever—we even locked it)
and then,
with love-giggles and love-touches
and finally
love's groaning union and eruption,
we made love again.

Nothing was different.
It was the same as always.

Taiwan Sketches

In 1986, I traveled with a children's choir to Taiwan, Republic of China. My time-touched and sagely apathetic presence in the midst of such young, energetic, and talented people was the result of twenty-odd years of three-chord, "Cripple Creek," hillbilly banjo playing. I believe it was my fireworks accompaniment of "She'll Be Comin' Round the Mountain" performed with the group at local concerts that cemented the relationship between this grizzled picker and the wholesome and harmonious chorale—and paid my ticket to twang internationally.

As my responsibility on this voyage was limited to showing up for performances and man-handling my banjo, my guitar, and sundry items of equipment associated with the amplification of my syncopated melodies, I enjoyed more freedom than the other adults in our entourage whose duties each included the twenty-four-hour supervision of two or three young people. In other words, while they were doing bed checks, I was doing night markets. It wasn't exactly fair, but then, to my knowledge, none of them could play the banjo either.

Following are written sketches taken from a green spiral notebook I carried on the trip, and recollections written since my return.

Taipei Morning

Six-thirty morning sunshine upon the ever-active streets. Wearing straw hats and big galoshes, the carwash ladies with buckets and hoses toil upon the Toyota fenders of taxicabs. The persistent, nasal buzz of motor scooters speaks through the alleyways and in droves at stoplights on the main boulevards. The rain last night was strong and the smell of sewage has diminished.

Children are coming out of apartment buildings and heading for school. First one little guy with his blue-shorts, white-shirt uniform steps into the alley and adjusts the weight of his backpack. He starts walking and others join him. At each intersection, as he waits for the crossing guards to blow their whistles and signal him to cross, more and more kids come: boys in their blue shorts, girls in blue skirts and white blouses. Everyone wears a backpack. Like the gathering of raindrops into brooks and streams, the flow of children increases at each intersection and moves on in a river of uniformed little students laughing and talking yet diligently progressing toward the wide gates of the school yard.

As I walk I, too, am swept along by the flood—carried by its current, only to beach myself as the river makes its final turn and disappears into the entryway of the four-story schoolhouse. There are teachers waiting and they smile at the children as they walk into the building.

At the gate a little girl with bright eyes and shining black hair climbs down from the back of her mother's bicycle and starts to run to join the others and disappear into the doorway. I take a picture. The mother doesn't approve and gives me a stern look. I apologize with my eyes, and she flashes a forgiving smile and rides back down the narrow street. There is the ringing of a bell. The street empties of child-sounds and movements, and returns to racing scooters, motorcycles, and horn-blowing taxicabs.

One morning I watched a man frying eggs on a gas grill mounted on a street cart. His business was located on a sidewalk where a small alley intersected with a wide and busy boulevard. I watched the artful movement of his spatula as he turned the eggs. There were people gathered about the cart patiently awaiting their breakfasts. His wife sold the eggs and pieces of bread while the man cracked more eggs and spread them upon the canvas of the black grill and, with grace and finesse, created a beautiful, yet never-finished painting.

Travel Sketch: Taipei to Hualien

This day there were holy moments along the train route down the east coast to Hualien. There were miles of shop-cluttered suburbs sprawling eastward along the rails out of Taipei. In all directions were concrete, cliff-dwelling apartment buildings where, upon balconies, imprisoned by trellises of metal, there were flowers growing and they were bright and beautiful and vividly alive. Beyond the city, in clearings cut from the dense, subtropical hillside vegetation, there were ornate and isolated shrines. In the eyes of laborers who toiled along the tracks with heavy burdens supported by bamboo shoulder poles, there were glimpses of the persistence of the human spirit. In town after town were stark, concrete-walled schoolyards filled with playing children. Beneath the bridges were women kneeling in shallow stream beds washing clothes. There was the great Pacific Sea and upon it were fishermen standing up in boats with skilled balance rowing through the roll of the near-shore surf.

Unfinished, Un-Mailed Letter

June 19, 1986
Hualien, Taiwan, ROC

Carol and Kristin,
　　There is no suitable place to begin any of this so I'll just tell what comes to mind. I'm having a few fine Taiwan Beers this afternoon, so bear with the condition of the mind from which these words are cast. A short time ago, while the troupe was resting up for a tour of a marble factory (needless to say, I passed on that one), I walked down to the harbor and, beyond the ships and the sea wall, lay the Pacific Ocean. To the east! All my life this body of water has stretched ever westward, and now I have physically disproved the myth of its infinite reach. There is something disillusioning about this obvious discovery. It makes me wonder about the whole wide universe and its other shore.
　　Anyway, as I philosophically wandered this lovely sea town contemplating the clay feet of physical reality, dozens of people—two, three, even four at a time on single motor scooters—buzzed by me shouting with smiling faces, "Hello!" And I shouted back and I loved it. The Chinese people seem fascinated with me. Thus far on this trip I have yet to see a beard as big and fuzzy as mine on either Oriental or Occidental face. People stop me and ask to take pictures. I get to hang on to the prettiest girls while their boyfriends snap pictures of them with the fur-faced American. It's all very gracious and warm spirited. When they get their Fujicolor prints back, there will be the image of a genuine and heartfelt smile upon the face of the, hopefully, not too ugly American.
　　Most of the children with whom I have come in contact are shy and they giggle, covering their mouths with their hands. But they are not afraid, and we usually establish some gestured communication that neither they nor I fully understand, nor will ever forget.
　　There has been a major exception, though. Yesterday in Taipei, as the little ambassadors of song ingested course after course of strange concoctions of ill-defined flora and fauna back at the hotel dining room, I was blocks away, gleefully up to my eye sockets in a Big Mac. Just as I was finishing the last of my golden crisp French fries and considering another wonderful round of McDonalds grease and beef, a tiny little girl seated across from me caught sight of my whiskers. She immediately wrinkled up her cute little face, clamped

shut her eyes, and, screeching like an exotic bird (or a male Chinese opera singer), buried her face in her mother's bosom—there to remain, I assume, until long after I had made my hasty departure.

Today, as I walked back from the harbor and the ships and the great (though finite) ocean, among the rushing motor scooters and the push carts with fresh fruit and handmade jewelry, and beneath the green mountains that climb steeply to the west; I was feeling fantastic. I walked past an elementary school and a whole class of dinky little smiling kids wearing identical blue and white uniforms pressed into an open doorway, and, in joyful discord, sang out a chorus of "hello's." I laughed and returned their greeting with a hearty "Hello!" and a wave and their arms were flying and they were laughing and even their teacher, in her spring-beige dress and her schoolgirl hair, smiled a pretty glance at me as she herded them back into the courtyard.

I'm going to walk up the street and buy a couple more beers. Perhaps I'll get back to this letter later...

Snake Alley and the Red-Light Ladies

The prostitutes looked so young they could have been school girls.

Last night I walked down a red-light street and saw them there, dozens of them lined up in front of street-stall whorehouses. They wore fancy dresses like young girls used to wear to dances or to church on Easter Sunday. In white and lacy, long fancy dresses and with their gleaming black hair and red lipstick, they stood in regiment in the entryways along the dimly lit alley.

The red-light district is adjacent to the infamous and hideous street known as Snake Alley. There, shouting men, reminiscent of carnival barkers, amuse clusters of onlookers by first tantalizing and then cutting the heads off of live snakes and turtles and bleeding them to make blood potions to supposedly enhance the sexual potency of male customers. The bright red blood was lined up in shot glasses; cocktails were available for those who chose to dilute their poison.

It's all very convenient. A desperate man can down a shot of snake's blood to charge up his weakened libido; then just walk a short distance and hire a lady of the night to accommodate its discharge; and, finally, take a few more steps down another alley and visit a VD clinic to remedy the effects of its use. All of it is there in ghastly clarity, all of the rudiments of sex, devoid of humanity.

Earlier on the trip, while in Chiai, we were accompanied by a group of students and their teachers from the Concordia School. The girls were all wearing pink blouses and gray jumpers. When they spoke their careful English to us, their eyes were bright with interest and they were so lovely in their modesty and in the spontaneity of their innocent faces. The teachers looked young as well, often only distinguishable from their students by the difference in their attire. When they spoke to me and we laughed together about small and polite matters, I perceived them in terms of a soft and sensuous grace, the pretty teacher-ladies of Chiai.

And in that night in Taipei, right down the block and off in a side alley from the sideshow decapitators of reptiles, could well have been sisters of the schoolgirls and teachers of Chiai. They looked so young and, yet, so vacant—like mannequins dressed for a church party. Cruelly scrutinized by the hardened gaze of pimps and madams, they stood awaiting the whims of any passing creature. Their eyes were glazed and unseeing, deadened by drugs or fear or, perhaps, solely by the devastating effect of red-light shadows and the snake-blood taste upon the lips of drunken men.

Hung by string nooses and skinned while yet they quivered in the throes of death, were the victims of Snake Alley.

The Buddha-Man

The Buddha-man sat cross-legged next to the curb of the filthy street. His shaved head was slightly bowed, his orange robe spread about him; he fervently mumbled a chant as his fingers ceaselessly worked their way through the infinite progression of the circular string of prayer beads he held in his hands. Passers-by dropped money into a bowl sitting on his lap and each time he interrupted his words to give thanks with a nod. He never once looked up; his stoic countenance never varied.

I gave him money; he acknowledged my offering. I stood on the sidewalk behind him and listened to his mind.

While the intense confusion of the night market incessantly milled about us, we meditated. As the monk moved his beads and chanted the holy words of his ancient and life-disciplined technique, I breathed the measured air of my own meditation—inhaling slowly, deeply, exhaling through the extremities of my being through the soul-portals of my eyes, my mind.

I listened. I listened to the mind-spirit of the Buddha-man.

I cannot write what I heard that Taipei, street-market night with its blowing horns and chattering merchants.

There are no words for such a silence.

... And

And there was Toroko Gorge with its narrow, one-lane road climbing up the chasm edge all the way to the clouds; and there were the throngs of people who crowded the stage in Koahsiung and again at Taipei, seeking autographs and expressing such appreciation with their smiles and their eyes; there was the heart-wide welcome of the County of Chiai; and there was the giant Buddha near Tiachiung, eighty feet high and black against the gray sky, where you can climb the spiral staircase innards, past the little incense shop and the religious displays, right up into the head and look out at the courtyard far below through the eight-inch-diameter nostrils of God.

And there was—in the movement, the smells, the sounds of the cities; the lushness and power of the mountains; the uniqueness of the cultures—a sense that the world is a vast and exotic place.

And, also, there was—in the laughter of the children, the friendliness of the people, and the view of daily life as a place of work and family and belief—a sense that this vast planet has elements which transcend diversity and connect us all as dwellers in a singular and spiritually unified human community.

Only When: The Mission of Art

"...art connoisseurs have been clamoring
for his abstract expressionist paintings."
    "Sunday Magazine," *The Rocky Mountain News*

(Photograph: The artist, looking almost sheepish,
adjusts his sunglasses.
Behind him looms his wall-sized canvas of smudges
and lines radiating the arrogance of ego aloof of
comprehension.)

Only when—
with color and line, form and texture,
metaphor of juxtaposition,
irony of assemblage,
intensity of clarity,
the communicative extension
of perception by imagination—
artists have quintessentially captured
for a world to experience:
the diamond-flashing lives of sun-crested rivulets
flowing through the sky-pierced caverns of the forest,
the ambience of ruddy-faced barrooms
and the essence of smoke-stained air,
the lips of lovers and the hands of toil,
the devil-spiced eyes of park-playing children,
the cracked faces of moribund forms
shawl-wrapped and huddled upon
the weather-gray ruin of ancient porches,
the color of a single instance of the sky,
the flow of time's sweeping wash...

Only when—
with passion and skill—
artists have honestly projected
the shape and shadow,

the immortality of infinite moments
and frozen them in oil or ink
or chalk or stone or word
or tone
upon the plane of human access,

should a culture embrace petty musings
of talent without form or comprehensible voice,
and bestow upon them
the Holy-Human Spirit's blessed designation: Art.

Convention at Casper / October, 1988

So, who would gather with me in this abandoned playground?
Autumn's touch thrills the sun-daunting winds,
the trees shimmer golden in the bursting prominence of their
impending demise,
there are no clouds this Wyoming afternoon,
and, thankfully, no children clattering
the swing-set chains
or shrieking shrill childsongs
down the polished slide to the
graveled earth.

So, who would gather here with me—
a solitary poet seated
at a sheltered wooden picnic table,
shaded from the sun's glare,
edged by the blind, chilling winds
that tell the certain promise of season's change?

A "poet" I call the grizzled form
who crafts these lines—
a pauper laboring for the worded art;
a mind and heart and soul-toiler seeking manna
from the capricious grace of the muses;
one who,
through lifetimes of joyous and tragic encounter
with the happenstance of being,
willingly collects the full force
of life's harsh and musical truths
and, in array of song-told expression,
daily, or by moments, or even heartbeats,
confronts what well could be a Universe or,
just as easily,
a rain puddle's reflection of a fool.
And, hearing the rowdy laughter of the Gods,
one who fears no mocking abuse

and lifts great draughts of mirthful brew
to the blackness and the hilarity—
the infinity of it all,
and speaks a toast each living instant
to the call of death
and immortality.

A poet, Priest of the heart-driven word:
And who would gather with me here?

Strange.
There must be legions at least
who would forsake dreary tasks and
join me in this distant corner of an empty park
in celebration of time's cruel and wondrous gifts
of seasons upon seasons,
souls upon souls.
And, yet,
throughout the glorious respite
of this afternoon stolen,
it is only by the imagined speaking
of the wording winds
through the crisp finality of October leaves,
and by the reverberation about the tin roof
of this small shelter
of my own wild-shouted poems
that I share the realm of another human voice.

Economics

A big man with a tiny baby sat at the restaurant table with an older couple. As he listened to the conversation, he gently tossed the child around with his strong hands and she made happy baby sounds. The old man talked of old times and his wife nodded verification to the tales and the young father listened while lovingly jostling his baby.

"Well, kid, we'd better go take care of the horses, hadn't we?" he said, and the child made small, laughing sounds.

The old lady went to the restroom while the old man finished his story. On the way back to the table she paid the waitress.

The tall man carrying his little baby got up and headed for the door. He stopped at the cash register and then turned to the old couple, tipped his hat, and said, "Thanks."

He left and the old man said to his wife, "I don't think he's got any horses left to take care of."

"I know," she said.

Crisp-fried Bacon

Outside is a winter's gloom-chilled morning.
Inside, a warm-stove kitchen.
It is a child's fresh day.

The taste and crunch of this bacon.
I am five years old.
I am forty-five years old.

Time aches within me this winter's day,
time and the ghosts of crisp bacon.

The Black Brew Coup

From somewhere across the scattered Aprils of my life comes a recollection.

I recall a spring day in 1963 when there was a baseball game to be watched and a personal rebellion to be enacted.

It was a Tuesday, and my afternoon classes were over by 1:30. Instead of rushing to the dormitory for a much needed, lengthy session of study, I barged into the room of my buddy, Luther Barden, and convinced him to interrupt his studious scholastic endeavors and take me to the 7-11 for a six-pack of beer.

I was an eighteen-year-old freshman at the University of Richmond, a Southern Baptist college where "the presence of alcohol upon your person, either carried or ingested" was cause for immediate expulsion from the venerable institution.

To hell with it. I didn't get along with those holy bastards anyway.

Luther, good friend that he was, didn't approve of my plan, but he had a car and was twenty-one years old and was immeasurably in debt to me for correcting certain of his personality flaws over the seven months of our acquaintance. "Come on, Luther," I prodded. "Just think of what a prick you were going to be if you hadn't met me."

By damn, yes! I would have some beer for my baseball game.

Nobody of any importance really gave a damn about baseball at the University of Richmond and, thus, home games were played upon an athletic field where there were no stands or fences or admission charges. I loved the baseball games and would sit upon a terrace beyond right field and waste away such would-be serious afternoons.

And so it was this fine April of my recollection. While the Richmond team, regardless of my solitary hoots and shouts of encouragement from the distant terrace, narrowly averted victory, blowing the game with Harvard in the final inning; I drank my six-pack of spring's dark and bitter brew—bock beer—from a cup and for all the notice of the world it looked just like Coca-Cola.

What pleasure there was that sun-wild, stolen afternoon to watch the Baptists play their game while quaffing my illicit beer before the very sight of their killjoy god and his legions of student narcs.

96

Fear at Dusk

Of late, there has been a time each day, as evening and darkness approach, when patterns of shadow and dimming light fill my soul with anxiety that nearly extinguishes my will.

I experienced similar bouts of apprehension when I was nineteen and out on the highways hitchhiking the nation. Night would approach, and I would feel so far from home. In the hour of daylight turning toward darkness, there are primitive senses triggered by the tones of the sky and the chill of air that tell the creatures of day they must find shelter against the perils of the night. I was nineteen and alone along some empty, distant highway and so far away from light and warmth in the gray of a homeless twilight.

But now I am not homeless. I am only alone. I can stoke the woodstove and drive out the cold. I can switch on the lights and dispel the gloom. I can play Beethoven on the tape machine and distract the howling winds. But for all of my efforts, there is little solace for the distance to which I have cast my soul in the quest of a few simple poems.

A Poet's Charge

Poet, Priest of Communication,
driven by the curse/blessing
of your Cosmic Mandate,
ever threatened
by the mortality of your tentative
step upon the small planet,
mightily fragile
in the emotional jeopardy
of your wild and vulnerable heart,
and constrained by the madness of
speaking glimpses of the Infinite
with the crude voice of a man:
turn up the collar of your
denim vestment
against the chilling draft of indifference
and give them
another poem today.

Dialing America: Radio Reflections

While extensively traveling the back roads of this nation, I listen to the radio.

I have listened to the clichés of AM talk show psychologists, and to the "Praise the Lord" promises of begging preachers; and to the FM multiplexed voices of lying politicians and profit-seeking prophets and philosophers of greed. I've heard the songs of adolescent rage, motel love, and hopeless self-pity; the screaming lies of better laxatives and low, low down payments. I've heard the hourly news, the "Good News," the analysis of the news, and, thank you, Paul Harvey, I've heard the "... rest of the story." I've been bombarded by two-for-one pizza scams; hell-or-heaven God cons; rebate rip-offs; once-in-a-lifetime wonder deals; and countless $19.95 record, tape, or compact disc collections of such classics as "Mairzy Doats." I've heard the outrageous and dangerous banter of election-year rhetoric. Bebopping "oldies," hate-howling "newies" and ten-thousand variations of a three-chord rendition of "You've left me here with my fly open," have rocked and waltzed and shuffled their way through the magic of the airways to the embattled countenance of my awareness.

Not that there is anything wrong with "Lambs eat oats and does eat oats and little lambs eat ivy.... " or pounds of pepperoni pizza or, hey, I wouldn't mind driving something a little more plush perhaps with a bit more punch than this nine-year-old Datsun of mine.

But it would seem from the ads and the sermons and the songs and thirty-second political pitches, that all we are is a nation of gimmicks, frustration, and lies. There is so much more sleaze than love, so much more beat than melody, so much more merchandise than heart shouted and sung and whispered insidiously by the electronic voices of this country.   So much more gloss than substance in matters of the mind, the body, and the soul.

It would seem by this transcontinental sampling of radio fare that the promise of the human spirit has been grievously diminished by the pettiness of fear and the complacency of local comfort. We can't let that happen, can we? Now, do you suppose I can find National Public Radio out here in the hinterland?

Not Just Another Day

   It was a winter morning and daylight was so late coming that the blackness and starlight and chill of night would accompany me on my daily trek down the mountain to work. I didn't mind the darkness or the shivering search for good-morning socks. It was worth it to live an hour's distance from the city. Outside my cabin door, I paused for a moment before beginning the rush for civilization. Looking at the sky I laughed at the Greeks and their contrived constellations—stellar, dot-to-dot soap operas. My gaze lowered and swept out over the pre-dawn plains spreading eastward beyond the forest and clearings of my mountain, and I thought about how each little speck of light represented a home, a family—indoor plumbing! I laughed again and my ancestors joined me, the primordial poets who in eons past stole Beer from the Gods and Love from the Loins and made the first Whoopee Cushions from the bladders of saber-toothed tigers.
   "Not just another damned day!" I shouted down the long white meadow.

Cribbage

Cribbage.
I saw the cards and the partners
and the pegs that moved up and down
the holes in the board.
Partners:
an intelligent young man
with a youth-foolish aura of certainty;
and a lanky drunk seeking a target
for his own self-hatred;
a soft, tall man with eyes and manner
telling of a compromised yet acceptable
peace;
and an ancient player of the fate-told board
whose crisp essence was a thing of
wit and stamina and, of course,
death.
The cards were dealt,
the pegs were moved,
the beer was drunk
and, finally, losers were established.
The old man and his gentle co-victim had lost.

I watched as they departed the booth—
losers standing to accommodate the seating
of new challengers,
winners standing to strut and stagger
to the men's room.
I saw them and they must have played
for several hours and drunk many beers
because, as they departed the booth,
all but the old man stumbled in imbalance
and moved about on uncertain footing.
All but the old man, in glib and drunken movement,
laughed their wins and losses

toward other games.

(He had little remaining hair
and the profile of his face was recessed and worn.)
The old man, with his many years,
walked steadily to a seat at a nearby table.
He smiled because luck had been a near thing
and because there was honor
in the movement of cribbage toward uncertainty,
regardless of winning or losing.

I watched.
New games started, new games finished.
Nobody held the table long.
Too drunk and too sure
lost to the team of silence and experience,
and silence and company
lost to the team of blind luck.
The old man watched, too,
and I saw him return from the bar
with a short draught in his left hand
and I saw the lady
who would laugh the bar full of her laughter
lean back for more clear, funny air
and just barely nudge
the edge of his shadow-passing form.
I watched as he tripped.
The old man who had walked confidently
beside those whose feet were tangled in table legs
and whose movements were a clumsy, drunken waltz.
The old man who had lost but by the kiss of fate,
who had laughed with the angels and devils
of near-death in every moment,
I saw him stumble and pitch
toward the humility of the cigarette-cratered carpet.
I watched.
"Joe," spoke the suddenly serious lady of hilarity,
and all who watched drew breaths of silent prayer
as the old man descended.

There was a chair

and Joe had the reflexes of a survivor.
He grabbed the chair
and didn't fall to the floor.
He only stumbled.

I watched.
All of the players had faltered in their stride,
but only the old man blushed, feeling like a fool.
Only the old man quieted the tavern
with his blunder.
Only Joe, the old man, knew—
and he told it so clearly with his blushing—
death without winning
is such an embarrassment.

Only the old man
fully knew the jeopardy
of carelessly playing the game.

As Simple as the Moon, the Answers of the Night

At the settling of dusk,
I was yet far up into the distant realm of a mountain valley.
Hastened by the deepening threat of darkness,
I quickly descended the path along the
rock-and-water voiced wonder of Three Mile Creek
toward home.
Sensing the ancient presence of the nearing night,
I spoke to a Spirit, asking, "What can you tell me?"
Distracted by the sound of my own voice,
I stumbled upon a shadow-hidden stone,
all but sprawling upon the trail.

And the Spirit said:
I can tell you to watch your step.

As a seeker of answers
to the ultimate questions,
to this trite revelation,
miffed, I spat back at the mocking night,
"I'll just do that."
But, then, humbled by the impotence of my outburst
and knowing it was not only the diminishing light
that had made me desperate,
from a heart that pulsed a despairing soul,
I shouted to the dimming heavens and
the ever-listening mystery of the trees,
"Spirit, what can you give me?"

And the Spirit said:
I can give you moonlight
upon this elusive trail.

Disheartened by the obvious, I asked no more.
And it wasn't until the darkness had made phantoms

of the jutting rocks,
and the grace of creek-gathered pine groves
had become a conspiracy of wind-shifting shadows,
that I began to grasp the immensity
of Spirit's white-glowing gift
flowing through the forest before me.

As simple as the moon, the answers of the night.

Smallchild #2

I watched as she played about the tavern
manipulating coin-less pinball machines,
vacantly rolling the cue ball
the length of the pool table and
watching it return,
occasionally giggling
loudly
without apparent cause,
and waiting for her father to finish his beer.

Though equally touched by God-golden sunlight
and the thrilling chill of winter's northern breath,
born of love's lusting unity
and flesh's miraculous garden,
twenty years nourished
by heart and lungs and love
and Kellogg's Frosted Corn Flakes
and pizza,

There are such small shoes
upon her feet—velcro fastened)…

"She'll ever have the mind of a child,"
I heard her father whisper.

Goddamn! It isn't fair.

The Sixteenth Street Mall

Drinking beer in a foreign land.

The Sixteenth Street Mall, Denver, Colorado. Inside the Paramount Cafe.

Four-dollar Budweisers and waitresses who look like my lovely, nineteen-year-old, California niece and who have fallen prey to this moment's stuttering, communicative crutch: the prefacing of nearly every thought or notion with the word "like."

"If you'll -like- wait a few minutes, I can -like- seat you at -like- a table out on the -like- mall."

"Thank you," I reply. "I'd like that."

The music here is piped from the depths of hell, and the bartender, even in his ridiculous youth, already affects boredom with humanity and its exciting women and intricate fascinations.

* * * *

At last! The like-waitress has found me a table out on the mall.

It is a different place out here—though the synthetic ambience of the inner sanctum has its reach, just beyond a flimsy, metal fence surrounding this outdoor region of the cafe, there is a much more diverse and greater parade to watch.

There are stylish people sitting about me conversing in the warm, spring sunlight while nibbling onion rings and sipping Long Island ice teas. Out on the sidewalk the world passes by in random array of young couples; shutter-clicking coveys of Japanese tourists; sets of steroid-popping, muscle-guys; an old lady curled over like a question mark—each step a stumbling fall toward the inevitable pavement; pairs of stroller-pushing mothers and fathers with massive diaper bags; sad creatures who search the trash cans for morsels of survival; people paced by purpose and others in ambling indifference to destination; people lost to the prospects of either purpose or destination; show-humans who in strutted stride step upon their well-quaffed poodles and make them yelp; and out there somewhere, the pretty lady for whom I wait with the patience of another full bottle of beer and a festival of humanity to ingest.

107

Return to the Night Diner

("Night Diner" is a poem of dream-death
as perceived in the eyes and heart-empty aura
of a beautiful, young waitress
working in an all-night, roadside restaurant.)

I see by her finger that she has married;
(It's been a year since I last sat here
sipping coffee and witnessing the corpse-cold
presence of the ghosts of hope deceased.)
I see by her smile and by the light and jovial
ambience she spreads along the counter
that she is not dead.
Poets can't be liars,
(I truly mourned the death of dreams)
but poets can be wrong—
or maybe moments are forever,
and we people just move on through
immortal layers
toward some local address called "death."
She is so much prettier this night
than when last I saw her and had to flee
her morbid specter—
her face has found a smile,
her voice a song.
She no longer threatens my dreams.
It is something wonderful
to watch her dance-free step and
willing touch.
She is not dead.
The profundity of death has been
supplanted by the sacred,
local imperatives of survival.
Now she is so much prettier,
though not nearly so beautiful as before.

Beauty is so much more absolute...
But, to hell with my precious poetic depth.
It is good to see her flourish
in this night diner/graveyard of dreams.
Her death would have been the death of us all.
Live on, pretty Karen,
that we all might
have this midnight breakfast
and, perhaps,
another night with which to dream.

"More coffee?" she asks me
with a smile that transcends
the tragic truths of poetry,
and I almost spill my cup
in the eagerness of my acceptance.

The Puritan Witch Ethic

So, where do the witches come from—
the ghouls, the ghosts, the grave-telling banshees?
Where did the awful things begin that stretch across
centuries to grip our hearts with cold, clasping
shivers of fear?
Out of darkness.
Yes, out of lightless realms
of unbridled night
come torments of the soul.

And, the way it was
when first came the Pilgrims...
It was written
in those early, Plymouth days:
"When we arrived in the New World,
there were no friends
to meet us;
no houses; nor, much less,
even a town...."
And when the sun was gone,
when the heat was drawn away
to the untold western sky,
and the deep-creviced chill of night
enwrapped the work-weary flesh
of frail humanity
in crude-clustered
cottages
huddled beneath the groping limbs
of stark trees,
when day sifted away
to gray dusk
and to sable-suffocation of night,
it got dark.

And then, to the unstill minds
of the pious and the pure,
by creaking moan of wind and limb
and shudder of ghost-gusted fear,
came stirrings frightful—
shadowed essences
long-buried
but never really dead.

From the rustling, the shrieking,
the harsh voices
of winter-bleak New England woods,
there came
a calling to the horrors
of the hidden mind—
the wickedness
deeply secreted
but ever-lurking
within the very soul
of the Puritan being.
Beneath the black and starless sky
of New World night,
they lay in rough-hewn beds
and listened to the
crackling of beasts,
the hideous laughter of devils,
the crisp whispers of creatures
ever dwelling
within their own hearts.

And then there were witches.

Oh, how the pure people
from England did sail,
to flee from all evil
but to little avail.

Through nightmares of darkness
they'd awaken at day,
and know even in sunlight
that evil would stay.

For the devil was ever
a-foot in the night,
to tempt Goodwife or Good-husband
with wicked delight.

Witch women, witch children,
witch farmers to blame,
and hang by their witch-necks
or burn in the flame.

Geronimo's Warriors

Ghosts upon the desolate reach
of the Arizona desert.
Listen to the coyotes howling,
know the madness of the moon.

Perhaps... When Death
(precludes the mention of another mortal day)

I have, of course,
the night sky,
and there is a stream.

I have considered stellar reaches
and the local eternity of ceaseless waters.

And I have perceived,
beyond the transient realm of mortality,
a sense of promise,
purpose,
extension,
connection.
I hear it in the flow of the
ever-falling waters.
I glimpse it
in the chill-shimmering
sphere of the night sky.

Though philosophy gives no solace
for loneliness
(We are all,
it seems,
so very young here in the venue
of light-spiraling millennia
and trickling brooks.)
and petty logic
fails the heart,
and though sorrow has its mocking intimacy
and tears make bleary
the lucid visage of the stars,
clearly,
I can tell you
there are voices and touches of the Infinite

in the loving might
of each human spirit.
I hear them
in the whispers of an ancient creek.
I feel them
in the night-echoes of my own solitude.

The Garden

When Eastern Kentucky was yet a young time and cars were hardly more than carriages; when early spring mornings were alive with mountain-glowing sunlight and the life-vibrant trickle of the waters of thawing woodlands; when the feuds had been quieted and the mines were open and were a steady place where a man, even if he wasn't paid an honest wage, could, at least, put in an honest day's labor; there lived in the valley of the Black Fork River a pretty mountain-child bride named Mary and her groom, Tyler.

Their small home, owned by the mining company, sat in a row with identical "Company houses" along the shallow, twisting river. Each square dwelling had a porch from which a sidewalk led to a front gate. Each had a fence surrounding a small yard. In futile struggle with the pall of coal smoke, annual applications of white paint upon wooden siding and fence posts were dimmed to a dismal gray. And high above the houses, spilling down the mountainsides at intervals along the valley, were the scars of stone litter strewn from the mouths of mines. Day and night, the valley would shake from the muffled boom of dynamite exploding deep within the heart of the mountain and from the bang of coal cars dumping black tons into the tipples. There was the sporadic pulsing of steam engines and the clatter and collision of the switching of coal cars. At night the sky was lit by the eerie-burning glow of ever-smoldering slate dumps as if hell itself were only a shovel's depth beneath the rubble.

They had come in late winter after a January wedding. Tyler's uncle was a fire boss at one of the mines and had arranged for the job and the house. Their people were farmers dwelling in another, more pristine valley on the far side of the mountains where corn was grown on the sides of steep hollows and pigs were kept in sties along the dirt lanes and chickens wandered freely about the random sprawl of outbuildings and farmhouses. Tyler was the youngest son in his family, and what land there was had already been apportioned to older siblings. He could either work for his father and brothers or cross the mountain and try it on his own in the mines. The choice, though difficult, had been obvious to both Mary and him.

So they left their families and the homes of their childhood and ventured into the realm of slate smoke and dynamite, poisoned streams, and growling industry. And, of course, once Tyler had overcome his unspoken anxiety about entering the ominous depths of the mines, and once Mary had quit flinching every time the mountain would rumble or the coal would avalanche down the chutes into the cars along the railroad tracks below; they both loved it. They were alone for the first time in their lives, and they had the security of their fresh, warm bed in which to delight and to enfold each other and make each other safe from the open-skied factory that was their new home.

She loved her small house, and, while Tyler turned his shifts at the mine, she moved about its four close rooms, touching them with her young energies and making them vibrate and sparkle in her love and vitality.

In the early day, when sunlight was only upon the highest ridges of the valley walls, shivering in the deep shadow of the mountain, she would walk to the gate with her man, and he would warm her in his arms until the gathering crowd of miners walking along the roadside would reach them. Then, with a quick kiss upon her soft lips, he would tear himself from her grasp to join the raucous grumble of the voices and laughter of the mob, the swagger of its stride, the lemming-like persistence of its momentum, and disappear down the curving highway. And each morning in those early days of her love she was never prepared for the chill of his departure and would shudder in the absence of his embrace.

Her days were happy but long in his absence. This was the special time in a marriage when two lovers can be an entire world. Days before the trials of survival and their economic exigencies regularly distract from the simple joys of love and touch, days before the incessant needs and blessings of children draw upon the selfish luxury of undivided love. There was excitement and adoration in the washing of his morning dishes, in the sacred making of their bed, in the dusting of their crude furniture. And her youthful movements about their home were a graceful dance, orchestrated by the ever-present music of her heart.

There are moments in the lives of most of us, somewhere in the chambers of careful recollection, as perfect as the early months of Mary and Tyler. It was their time to flourish in the fragile gift of love and ignorance that is the morning of a marriage, the dawn of the life-long day called adulthood. A time when, in the ephemeral intermingling of child's play and carnality, we do not yet feel foolish with our hearts and flesh.

Tyler worked hard in the mine. His rearing had made him accustomed to the toil of rugged farmland, and the transition from plow to pick was an easy one for him. He also knew that hard work made a quicker clock and relentlessly devoured the choking hours of his shifts in anticipation of the simple and sensuous joys of his bride.

Once the dishes were stacked in the high kitchen cupboards and the bed was taut with adoring perfection and the daily battle with the black dust had been fought with cloth and feather duster and the clothes rinsed clear and hung from the line and the black wash water had been cast from the back porch, she would put on her coat and walk down the highway to the Company Store.

It was March, and the season was turning young regardless of the persistent chill.

It was yet a time of frosted mornings and drizzling afternoons, but, in the young belief of Mary no lingering chill of winter's final, fitful utterances could dissuade visions of flowers along the front walk and vegetables growing green and plentiful beside the house and along the back fence above the river. She was a farm girl and she would bring life from the soil. Life in the form of tomatoes and corn, potatoes and snap beans. Life in the form of bright flowers and the smell of mint and dill.

Her purposes were fertile and she ached for the germinative warmth of spring sunshine. As she would frugally play the game of grocery shopping at the Company Store and carefully balance the bargain of potatoes against the flavor of stew meat, the necessity of bread against the tantalizing sweetness of rock candy; she would eye the corners of the barn-sized building for the appearance of seed.

Her clothing was simple, but her plain beauty made her elegant. When the shift whistle would shriek the length of the valley and the sable-faced miners wearily plodded the highway alongside the river, regardless of the weather she would be outside waiting for him. Sitting upon the chain-hung swing on the front porch, she would peer anxiously down the road for the first glimpse of her man's face in the rabble of denim and dust-blackened flesh. She was a flower herself, fresh and glowing with such life that even the most cynical of the old miners had to have felt a twinge of ancient and perfect memory at the sight of her. With jeers of good-natured farewell, in unceasing motion, the retreating shift would deposit Tyler at the front gate and mumble itself on in ever-thinning rank around the bend and out of sight and sound.

She couldn't touch him for he was filthy with the coal. There was a washroom off the back porch, and, as he entered it, she would carefully take the lunch pail from his outstretched hand. With white teeth and shining eyes piercing through a thick mask of coal dust, he would smile at his bride.

The work was terribly hard. Even though he was young and strong, it would exhaust him, and, after some sweet words and a long embrace, he would often doze off in the soft chair in front of the coal stove while she cooked dinner. It was a near-mythic time when no flaw could exist and, hence, when the water-thin broth lay as a puddle to the potatoes and home-canned green beans and tomatoes upon the evening's plate, and dessert was a slice of bread spread with homemade apple butter; it was a royal feast they enjoyed as they sat and laughed and loved across from each other at the kitchen table.

As all moments beautiful and sublime are eternal, and as all moments are eternally consumed in the instance of their being, such are the evenings and nights of young lovers—ever and simultaneously never existing: Elusive and filled with essences of pleasure and giggling laughter—invisible.

It was a time of great quilts in the Appalachians. A time when venerable old fingers could artfully stitch patterned scraps into wondrous thick bedding, and when, in circles of aunts and cousins and neighbor ladies, needles and thread and words frenzied in congresses of colored fabric and colored gossip. A time when no child born would ever want for winter wrap, and, particularly, no newly wedded couple would ever need to stay the drafts of damp seasons without barrier of soft and heavy quilts upon their bed.

And, though hints of spring had come to the daylight, winter still spoke through the night in howling winds across the high ridges and in sweeping chill against the thin walls and through the ill-fitted windows. And deep beneath layers of country quilts, Mary and Tyler would make love each night and be in love each night and cling to each other throughout the dreams and terrors of each night—quilted from the cool night air, quilted from the lightless night, quilted from the chill of remnant winter's death-cold touch.

"Tyler."

"You're going to ask about that damned garden again, aren't you?"

"Maybe..." she said as there was play and teasing laughter in her voice.

"It's too cold yet, Mary. The ground's just barely thawed."

"I hardly had to wear my coat when I walked to the store today."

"Hardly?"

"Yes, and the sun's coming up earlier and earlier every day. Summer's just around the corner, Tyler, and I don't even have the dirt turned yet."

"I'd probably bust the spade handle trying the break the ice."

"Tyler... "

"Besides, I'm too tired to be out fooling with a flower patch after a day of coal mining."

"You never seem too tired to take me to bed."

"That's different."

"Oh..."

"Yeah. You're not so skinny as a spade handle nor so cold as winter dirt."

They had eaten dinner, he had played his guitar for a while, and they had made love. No one had ever known a more perfect evening.

"I might cool off myself, you know."

"Is that a threat?"

"I don't know—when are you going to dig up my garden?"

Tyler sat straight up and in mock indignation shouted, "Where's the preacher!?"

She was laughing. "The preacher?"

"I just want to know where in the middle of all that 'honoring' and 'obeying' and 'I-thee-wedding' he said anything about gardening. Where's the license!? Get out the license—I need to be reading the fine print where it says your loving's got something to do with my shoveling."

"Tyler... " she said, and there was such seduction in the feigned trailing of her voice, "please dig up the ground for me."

"Mary, just imagine what it would feel like to be a little kernel of seed corn—stored in some warm feed shed all winter, sleeping in a big old bag with all your seed-corn buddies, dreaming dreams about the promise of summer and growing up to be a tall, straight stalk— and then when it's not even hardly March you get stuffed in a hole in the cold, cold ground. Can't you just feel the shiver of it?"

"Now you make me feel like a monster for even thinking of such a cruel and heartless thing as planting a garden."

"It is a bit frightening, when I think of it," said Tyler.

"Well, I'll show you frightening," she said, laughing as she attacked him in ferocious tickling charges. And he writhed in helpless hysteria at her deadly accurate jabs, for lovers always know where lovers are most ticklish. With work-hardened muscles rendered weak and tear-filled eyes pleading through shrieks of uncontrollable merriment, he cried, "I give, I give. Stop it, Mary. I'll do it, I'll do it."

"Do what?" she asked, poised above him with index finger pointed and ready to storm ribs at the slightest hint of insincerity— covers kicked to the floor, bare flesh blushed by the fervor of battle.

"You know," he said.

"Say it," she threatened with a feigned movement that curled him into a pitiable fetal ball. "Say it, Tyler," she said, pressing her warm skin against his quivering form, her face close, "Say it, or I'll show you no mercy."

He looked into the frenzied beauty of her face, smiled, and wrapped her in his arms. "Fear not, my love. Tomorrow, after work, I promise I will turn the earth for you."

* * * *

Listen to the mountain songs. Listen to the ballads, the sad poems sung to the mournful, bending of wind-telling fiddles. Listen to the tales of timeless grieving. Look into the ancient, Appalachian eyes of mountain women and know the heart of Mary on the morning of the garden that never was to be.

She had kissed him goodbye at the gate and had made him promise once more about the digging. She had watched him disappear around the curve as the mountain shook and the coal cars rumbled. She had washed the dishes and was stacking them in the high cupboards when she heard a knocking at the front door and suddenly felt foolish for the light song she had been singing. It was Tyler's uncle, and, by his terrible eyes, before a word was spoken she knew her man was dead.

It was Eastern Kentucky where it seems that men have always been killed in the mines and where their women have always been left weeping in the crude parlors of coal-grayed Company houses.

* * * *

At mid-morning the procession had started out from the farmhouse, the childhood home to which the boy had been returned from the ravaged valley of the coal. Pallbearers had loaded his coffin upon a large wagon drawn by a team of white horses. The sun was bright, and the sky clear. Next came a carriage in which Mary rode with members of their close families. Her clothing was black. She was hardly more than a child, and yet, it was time for her to bear terrible knowledge of the absolute finality of mortal loss.

The demands of the complex rites of custom and religion surrounding a death can produce a protective numbness in the awareness of those who suffer, but, just as chilling breezes daunted the facade of springtime that sunny March morning, realizations of emptiness shuddered through the courage of the girl and asserted themselves regardless of the intent of her resolve.

In Sunday suits and dresses, assembled in family clusters, the rural entourage walked behind the carriage and the wagon-hearse as they crept along the dirt lane up the rising meadowland to the wooden church on the hill. It was a bitter, cruel irony that where just short months earlier Mary and Tyler had been married was now to be a place of final farewell. It was heavy upon the hearts of all who saw her. There were many, young and old, among the solemn mourners who had known the bonding magic of early love, and they grieved with Mary as she traveled the black-clad journey to the cemetery.

They sang "Rock of Ages," and the preacher said, "... call upon Jesus in a time of need." They recited the "valley of the shadow of death." And the preacher said, "... home again with Jesus," and, "Praise God, he's home, he's free, his earthly trial, Blessed Lord, is over." There was the grave-side "dust to dust." Then they lowered Tyler's body into the earth.

It was a country churchyard on a chilled spring morning, and the farm people had gathered to bury their boy who had been lost to the mines. And, steadied by the firm arm of her father about her shoulders and by the gentle arm of her mother about her waist, Tyler's pretty bride watched through a blur of wet eyes and listened to the awful and indelible sound as brothers shoveled fresh dirt upon the grave-deep lid of a wooden coffin.

There was a final "Amen," and it was done. The knit of the mourners was broken, and in random clusters they wandered the meadow road back to the farm. There is an audible sigh at the closing of a grave and then the processes of survival commence in lighter conversations and fewer outbursts of weeping.

As she rode along in the carriage, there was a voice, perhaps spoken, perhaps only imagined—a voice that she alone could hear.

It was the voice of the distant howl of a soul-chilling wind and, over and over, it whispered, "Tyler's gone. Tyler's gone."

In the continuation of the ritual of healing, scores of friends and relatives arrived at the home of Tyler's family to comfort, to grieve, and silently to contemplate the mysteries of a God who would take the boy-man so soon.

The large dining room table was covered with hot dishes, platters of sliced meats, breads, soups, pies—with each arriving wave of mourners more food was deposited.

The day had warmed and the men stood talking in the yard. Some of the women were on the porch, some busied themselves in the kitchen. The children felt awkward in their special clothes. They wanted to play but knew they didn't dare.

Mary sat in a corner of the parlor and, through the front window, watched the lengthening shadows of the falling afternoon sun.

"Come on, honey. It's time to go home."

"Yes, Mama," she said.

Dusk was nearing and she pulled a blanket about her as the wagon headed down the road toward her family's farm.

"I want you to go right to bed when we get home. Time will start helping you mend tomorrow morning, but for now the best thing for you is sleep."

"Yes, Mama," she said. "I'll go to bed."

The night drew dark and the house quiet, and, alone in a large bed beneath the weight of patchwork quilts, she lay and thought of the shivering night winds and the persistence of winter in the damp, cold dirt. Her eyes were opened wide in panic and horror. With apprehension nearly stealing the breath from her, she thought of a kernel of seed corn freezing in the cold, cold earth, and she whispered aloud as she rose from the bed, "A seed too early planted." And to the empty room she spoke as she pulled on her shoes, "Tyler's in the winter-cold ground."

She gathered a quilt about her and quietly left the house.

* * * *

The gravestones were pale and ghostly in the light of the haze-filtered moon, and upon the mound of dirt that was the fresh grave of Tyler there was, smoothly spread, an Appalachian quilt. Mary lay upon the quilt and the dirt and the grave and shook with the cold and the grief and the loss.

It was the night of the day of burial, and upon the bed of the grave-shroud quilt the child lay sobbing in the cold light of the sky-veiled moon, and the silence of the churchyard was lost to the voice of her sorrow.

As slowly turned the hours of the moon, she lay—consumed by the futile madness of dispelling the frigid truth of death with but a blanket of hand-sewn cloth and the life-forsaken beating of a broken heart.

Then, sweeping down from the mountains and rushing through the churchyard, came an abrupt blast of a night-gusted, death-cold ghost of a winter's wind, scattering old leaves about the cemetery and tearing through the limbs of the yet barren oak trees.

Mary suddenly ceased her weeping and sat straight up. About her was the tumult of the wind and the swaying phantoms of monstrous trees and moon-cast shadows; the creaking of limbs, and the ghastly tilt of granite stones toward sunken graves.

She was not frightened. In grief there can be a distressing immunity to fear. And, though she shivered, she felt no cold, for sadness had numbed her to the petty play of the elements upon her flesh. But she no longer wept. Besieged by the howling rage of a dying season, with an intuition as old as the paths of mammalian beasts through the forests of the Appalachians, Mary sensed within her that she was not alone. Quieting her own desperate sorrow, she pulled the quilt about her and sat still, awaiting the morning.

* * * *

Early the next day they found her in the graveyard. She was chilled and shaken, but the tears were dry upon her face and in her eyes there was a newly-found resolve. Mary stood there in her nightgown and felt her mother's frantic embrace and heard the words, "Come on home, Honey."

"Yes, Mama," she said willingly. And as they stepped away, Mary reached down and grabbed a corner of the fallen quilt and pulled it from the grave. She wrapped it about her, and, as she held the quilt tightly against her abdomen she said, "It wasn't too early for our seed, Mama. We planted our garden just in time."

About The Garden

It was a late January when Mom died. The evening after the funeral, when Dad returned from walking the dog in the backyard, he was chilled. The old dog shook herself and headed across the room to curl up in her puppy bed near the hearth. My sister and I were concerned when Dad had nothing to say. He just sat down on the end of the couch.

You'd have to have known my papa to understand that, even in the most somber of times, he was seldom one to lose the spark of wit and optimism (and. okay, maybe a bit of self-denial) that drove him and any who were in range of his energies.

But the last couple of the forty-three years he was married to Mom had been difficult. Memory had abandoned her and left her as sweet as ever, but in constant need of his help. She would panic when he was gone to the store or down to the gas station or, toward the end there, when he was just in the next room. It was not until her final two weeks that she was admitted to a care facility and, by then, not much was left of either of them. I wrote about those days in an essay included in this book entitled "The Insensitive Man."

And by the final weeks, when her wonderful mind had gone from being partly cloudy to having the steel-smooth cast of a winter's day, and even her own childhood, her own history, had retreated to inaccessible realms of her fading mind; when even "now" had ceased to have focus—when all who loved her knew death was the only kindness left for her; he, too, had nearly wasted away in the struggle for the last days of her life and dignity.

My robust father was bone-thin and his voice a near-empty vessel by the time Mom died.

He was such a skinny old man sitting there silent and alone on the end of the couch that winter-chilled night of the day we had buried his wife.

My sister Nancy and I—it broke our hearts to see him there.

You can imagine my 1914-vintage, Great Depression-, WW II-era old man wasn't a big one for outward shows of emotion—with, of course, the life-long and infectious exception of laughter. Not a big weeper, my dad.

Nancy brought a blanket and wrapped it about him. She sat next to him and I settled on the armrest and then he just killed us. He shuddered so hard it spilled the tears from his bright old eyes and we fell upon him with more of our love than we had ever expected him to be able to know.

He gently set us both a-right and steadying himself, wiping his eyes with his hand, and clearing his throat, he said, "It's just so cold in the ground."

And then he told us the story of my mom's sister, Aunt Pricey— the child bride who lost her husband to the mines back in Eastern Kentucky in the nineteen twenties.

He said, "...and they found her up in the graveyard. She hated the thought of him being cold in the ground and took him a quilt up there. They found her on the blanket she'd spread out on his grave. So cold."

So, Aunt Pricey became half of my short story, "The Garden." Half the story, I say. There was another story blended to become this work of fiction that tells such a true story. A couple decades later, in the late forties, my dad's sister, Aunt Mary, was another young girl with a young husband and a life just beginning. It is an all-too common story. Some kind of a minor shift in the coal seam and Uncle Burl was gone in a crushing instant and Aunt Mary became a child widow. She never remarried. But neither was she ever really abandoned. Mary was four-months pregnant with my cousin David Burl when the accident took her man.

It is the way of Truth to wend its way through lifetimes to become the larger story that is art.

Dreams of Never; Dreams of Now

It was early in the heart of man
when sky-days spoke no doom,
when all the cries and all the lies
were futures yet to loom;

When fortune's quirks of fancy
were not yet things to fear,
when all the paths a day could take
brought life's front edge so near;

When sparkling sunlight, early up,
would glow the whole day bright,
and, though they'd scold, the voices old
would speak of hope and light;

When all the childhood days of time
were sung by old and young,
when no cliché could call the day
for words were fresh of tongue;

When idle was the pace of life
and summers seemed forever,
when giggles were a young girl's charm
and words of love were clever;

When fool-free were my fantasies
and daring were my dreams,
and full of frenzied wonder
I wrote poems in flowing streams;

I wonder of those heart-spun times,
aware of my own distortion—
I see those days through dreams' sweet haze
and know my mind's contortion.

Though truth to me I clearly see,
and a cynic's sight I've learned,
and life's long lessons every day
tell of the scars I've earned;

There's still a part of dreams alive,
an essence yet undying—
a spark of all those never times
to keep us old fools trying.

Comments (1990 Edition)

1. I wish to apologize for charging $7.95 for this book instead of an honest $8.00. It seems to contradict the honesty of poetry to use deceptive pricing, but commerce often contradicts the honesty of poetry.

2. "Encounter," "The Victory," and "The Garden" are works of fiction, however closely they might resemble events I have experienced and true stories I have heard. This fiction is a product of condensation, blending, and enhancement for the purpose of emphasis and clarity. I have included them because I know their messages to be true.

3. I wish to thank Andy, Vivian, and Sally at Network Graphics of Denver, Colorado, for their patience and support in turning an old mountain poet into an electronic typesetter.

4. Thanks to Albert Dreher, fine artist, for his masterful use of brush and watercolor in touching up the cover; and for his perceptive illustration of the effect of the High Wind.

5. I wish to express my appreciation to the R.L. Nichols (Senior) Bank of Woodbridge, Virginia, for financial and moral support in the production of this work. (Honest, Dad, this time I'm going to try to pay you back.)

Comments (2013 Edition)

1. Again, I must apologize for the deceptive nature of a price of the e-book,$3.99 instead of an honest $4. The policies of commerce aren't likely to shift toward the truthful in the span of my days. At least the print edition is a straight up $10.00.

2. It's interesting. The twenty-seven years that have passed since first I had this little work printed and made available for the world comprise at least a fourth or maybe even a third of my lifespan. In reworking these poems and stories and essays for re-publication I've given deep consideration to the truths I tried to tell back in 1990 and the truths I know this spring of 2017. I don't know much more, perhaps even less, but what I said, for what it was worth, is as true now as when I sat up there on the side of a Rocky Mountain in a tipi and edited and typeset them in the first place. I live in a real house now, I'm reunited with my lovely wife Carol, I've lost a bunch more white hair on top but have grown an even longer and more wild-assed beard. I'm decently healthy and hearty for an old guy. I don't drink beer or chase women anymore, but I still howl at the moon and converse with ravens on a fairly regular basis. It's a good life, but still dangerous to the open-hearted perception of a poet.

3. The world has spun itself into some real fixes in the past couple of decades. I thought I would be well clear of this planet before the greedy Oil Guys *et al* actually started frying it to a crisp with global warming. Wrong-o. And terrorism... back in 1990, I knew there were some hateful bastards out there but really had no grasp of the extent to which mad doctrine could twist the love of the Gods into such murderous fury. Hitler's still dead, right? You know, my friends, no matter how openly I have risked the full-force truths of poetic awareness in my life, there are occasions when events make me feel I have been naïve. Then I look back over these words and remember the reach of the night sky, the depths of love's touch, and the raw

power of Creation's rush through the portals of my soul and know I'm no fool to believe in Art, humanity, and even myself.

4. Well, the R.L. Nichols (Senior) Bank of Woodbridge, Virginia, has closed. July 7, 2011. Bless you, Papa. (Honest, I'm going to try to pay you back.)

Other Works by Robert Nichols

Most of these titles are currently published as e-Books available through all the major distributors. Also, printed editions are in process as books on demand. Gradually, I will get them out—hey, it's a lot of work.

Books etc.

The Kristin Book (1987)

Story of the first fifteen years of the life of my daughter who was born with Down Syndrome.

This book, reissued with an update, is now available in eBook format as *The Kristin Book: Update 2013*

Take the Aspen Train (1988)

Co-authored with Edward Larsh. Coffee table, Colorado history / social philosophy / train book. *(No longer available.)*

Adventures in the High Wind (1990)

Collection of my poems, stories, and essays.
eBook edition, 2013.

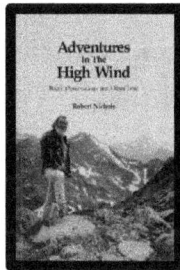

Leadville, U.S.A (1993)

Co-authored with Edward Larsh. Oral history of Leadville, Colorado. *(No longer available.)*

The High Priest of Hallelujah (1999)

Niche-less novel of poetic vision, humor, and satire.
eBook edition, 2015.

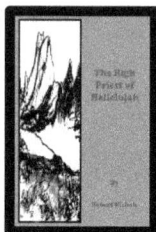

Summer Words, 2000 (2001)

Collection of short essays about laughter, God, knife throwing and much more.
e-Book edition, 2014.

God of the Poets (2003)

It took me twenty years to get this one right. When I finished the first version in '83 I didn't know enough to write my own novel. Perhaps now I do. I was pretty much just a stenographer for the real author, God. This isn't traditional stuff. It's a story of art, love, humanity and... *the purpose of life*.
e-Book edition, 2014.

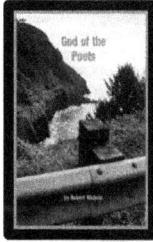

Albatross: The Curse of Honesty (2013)

The first novel I wrote, and re-wrote, and finally published. It's a funny and touching tale of a fellow whose life is nearly destoyed by the curse of absolute honesty.

The Great Book of Bob (2009)
The Great Book of Bob **eBook edition** (2014)

A unified collection of humorous, soul-wrenching, and harshly honest tales and thoughts gleaned from a lifelong love story— stories of a poet's love of sunrises, poetic epiphanies, laughter, and for the soulmate of his life. And the best part about it, it's not some icky-sticky, lovey-poo bunch of hearts and flowers. It's hard-edged wonder and real reason for all of us to be glad to be alive. I tell *my* stories that we may each realize the significance of our own.

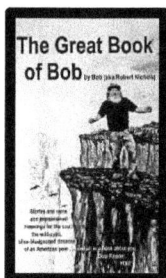

Uncle Bob's Big Book of Happy (2017)

I should make this clear from the start. None of this is easy. The first chapter of this work starts out saying exactly that: This will not be easy. I tell some hard truths. Don't be misled by the mirthful lilt of my title. Uncle Bob here will do his best to help you be happy, but none of this means diddly-squat if you can't face harsher aspects of our everyday journey. I write this book in hopes that my stories, theories, blathering bilge and sublime prayers may be of help to you in avoiding the burden, the curse of bitterness. It's no fun living in a world of bitchy whiners, angry jerks, and cranky bastards. You know what I mean.

THE FOOTLOCKER SERIES

This is a series of eBooks gleaned from fifty years of writing excavated from Robert Nichols' old footlocker of notebooks and scraps of papers—the repository of a life of art.
For information contact Robert Nichols at Mtmuse44@aol.com.

Titles:

about Time
about Mountain Living
about Seasons
about Paths

about Time: Poems and Other Stories (2015)

The first in the series—poetry, stories, and photography about ancient time, the time of children, the time of young adults, and the time of growing old. It's really not about time at all. This is a book about life.

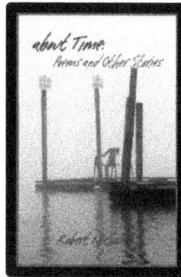

about Mountain Living: Finding a Way (2015)

A journey told in story and poem. A life trek from discontent and restlessness to commitment and discovery. This work tells of a succession of habitats and lifestyles progressing farther and farther from the city and further into a better destiny—from apartment to cabin to tipi to hilltop shrine of art, nature, and spirit. A journey from complacent certainty to out-on-the-edge primal survival. Perhaps my story will encourage yours. And, beyond the tale I tell, just read the poems and stories as the art they are intended to be. You will laugh and weep and contemplate—you will be changed.

about Seasons: the Wind and Weather of Our Days (2016)

Poems of the seasons—not just some cliché sweetness about leaves and blossoms either. This is the core stuff of being. Seasons, wind, and weather—the fierce and beautiful power of Nature that can keep us humble and exhilarated throughout our lives. It is the very "life and death" intensity of these metamorphic cycles that excites the turning of our years with risk and wonder. Time takes away our days, storms wash away our safety, seasons etch our flesh with danger. Old Spirits out on the plains once told me, "Earth shall never be tame... celebrate your fear and feel you are alive!" Yes!

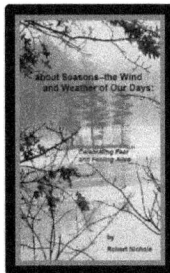

about Paths: Journeys Through Wonder, Danger, and Self (2017)

The fourth in the Footlocker Series of books, *about Paths,* is another collection of poetry and thought-provoking essays. I take you with me as I recount youthful journeys hitchhiking the country, express vignette word-sketches of people and places along the way throughout the years, and, hopefully give a sense of purpose to the paths all of us take.

Read these works and you will know the harsh and enlightening truths of the road, you will contemplate the ugly realities of American racism, you will observe the humor and pathos of the passing scene— you will travel with me, the path of an open-hearted poet.

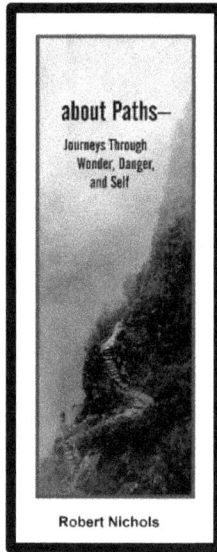

about Paths—

Journeys Through
Wonder, Danger,
and Self

Robert Nichols

CDs

Maybe Someday, 2000. Compact disk of original songs performed by the R-Man with the accompaniment of his "all-Bob band of alter egos." (The wonder of multi-track recording.)

Summer Words, 2000 CD version, 2007. Compact disk of readings from *Summer Words, 2000,* with original interlude music and a one-minute meditation chant by the Brothers of the All Bob Tibetan Choir.

Website

Website, 2013. Carol Nichols has compiled the decades of my life and art in a website titled: Carol's Friend Robert Nichols.

carolsfriendrobertnichols.com

And

One bumper sticker, 1978. "Like reading bumpers? Try a book."

LIKE READING BUMPERS ?
TRY A BOOK!
Right to Read

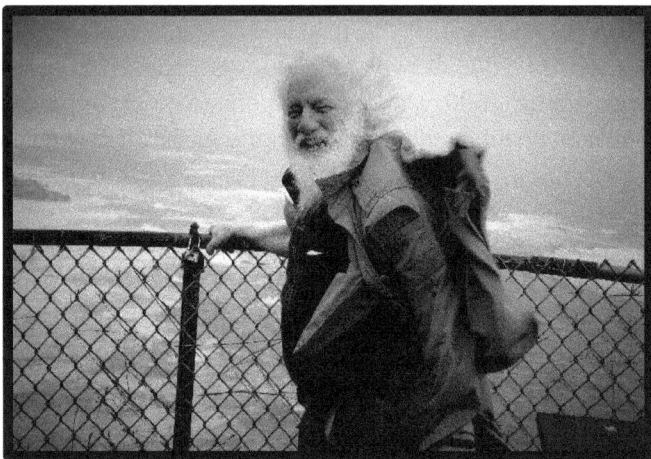

80 mph gusts up on Otter Crest

Robert Nichols writes, carves, sings,
and loves life
with his family in Oregon.

www.ingramcontent.com/pod-product-compliance
Lightning Source LLC
Chambersburg PA
CBHW060801050426

42449CB00008B/1472